"This guidebook transports the reader from awareness to action and ultimately victorious transformation. The author helps navigate past stumbling through the rubble of life's quakes to a highly accessible path of personal empowerment and joy. If you've ever experienced trauma or a harsh slap in your faith while remaining a silent victim, *Letters from a Better Me: How Becoming an Empowered Woman Transforms the World* gives you the power to finally speak in a brave voice and stand for what you believe in."

—*D. C. Stanfa*, author, *The Art of Table Dancing*

"I had the pleasure of reading an advance copy of *Letters from a Better Me: How Becoming an Empowered Woman Transforms the World*. What a FANTASTIC read! Rachael does a wonderful job of guiding the reader to take a look within and explore their own psyche. I love the format of the author's letters. These spur the readers to dive deeper into their own life experiences and thoughts. This book guides us to dig a little deeper, empower ourselves, and create positive change. It encourages the reader to be kinder and more understanding—which can only be of benefit to humanity. I highly recommend this book for your own bedside table and as a gift for someone you love!"

—*Sheila M. Burke*, bestselling author, *I Am What's Wrong*, and founder of Being Better Humans

"I am so impressed with Rachael Wolff and how she has taken what she's collected along the way and transformed it all into something we can all benefit from! She is a gift! What Wolff has done in her book, *Letters from a Better Me: How Becoming an Empowered Woman Transforms the World*, is create a process that permits us to be open, honest, thorough, and vulnerable. To own the pieces that comprise us. And, through reflection, to become our own catalyst for self-change. It takes a plan and it takes practice. An empowered woman knows how to empower other women. Through the experience exchange, we learn to hear clues that are a cry for help—first in ourselves, and then our sisters. Wolff has created a model that could very well break a cycle of good intentions and instead lead to change."

—*Kristie Kindstrom*, vice president, Wealth Solutions, Raymond James; co-chair of Women's Interactive Network at Raymond James

---

Becoming a strong woman starts with self-development, and Rachael Wolff's book is a powerful tool to help you soar."

—*Louise Harmon*, author of *Happiness A to Z*

_____

Letters from a Better Me: How Becoming an Empowered Woman Transforms the World provides a powerful roadmap for the journey from suffering to empowerment to peace. Personal and deeply passionate, Rachael Wolff's perspective-expanding wisdom, and loving insights, serve as an inspirational reminder of the following: 'I raise up my voice—not so I can shout, but so that those without a voice can be heard.'"

—*Bridgitte Jackson-Buckley*, author of *The Gift of Crisis: How I Used Meditation to Go from Financial Failure to a Life of Purpose*

_____

"*Letters from a Better Me* takes the reader on a complete journey from the depths of chaos to true empowerment. You will want to laugh, cry, shout, and chant. It is a must-read for the times we live in. Wolff helps the reader see deep down within to find the spark buried under years of misunderstanding. This is not only a book you will want to read, but a book you will want to pass down to the generations that come after you."

—*Becca Anderson*, author of *The Book of Awesome Women*

———————————

LETTERS FROM
A Better Me

LETTERS FROM
A Better Me

How Becoming an Empowered Woman Transforms the World

Rachael Wolff

Mango Publishing
Coral Gables

Published by Mango Publishing, a division of Mango Media Inc.

Cover Design: Jermaine Lau
Interior & Layout Design: Jermaine Lau

For permission requests, please contact the publisher at:

Mango Publishing Group
2850 Douglas Road, 2nd Floor
Coral Gables, FL 33134 USA
info@mango.bz

For special orders, quantity sales, course adoptions and corporate sales, please email the publisher at sales@mango.bz.
For trade and wholesale sales, please contact Ingram Publisher Services at
customer.service@ingramcontent.com or +1.800.509.4887.

Letters from a Better Me: How Becoming an Empowered Woman Transforms the World

Library of Congress Cataloging
ISBN: (p) 978-1-64250-140-7 (e) 978-1-64250-139-1

BISAC: SEL023000, SELF-HELP / Personal Growth / Self-Esteem

LCCN: 2019948830

Printed in the United States of America

Letters from a Better Me *is a contract to transform into the best version of you, shifting negative self-talk and blame into true empowerment. Release the negative emotional attachments that keep you from experiencing authentic love.*

Free the empowered woman within you and transform the world!

I dedicate this book to my soul sister/agent, my amazing family, and my supportive partner in love. All the love, support, lessons, and encouragement have made this journey more than I could have ever imagined. Thank you.

Table of Contents

Part I: Blinders Off

Part II: Acceptance of What Is

Part III: Taking Charge as an Empowered Woman

Foreword

Dear Fellow Answer-Seeker,

I was a reader of this book, just like you. I came here with my own blinders on, not even realizing the fear and negativity that bubbled just under my skin's surface. I worked my way through all nine chapters (nine being a super spiritual magical number!) and came out the other side feeling really cleansed.

In *Letters from a Better Me: How Becoming an Empowered Woman Transforms the World*, Rachael Wolff takes us through three stages of being: Awareness, Acceptance, and Action, through letters written to elicit reflection, emotion, and, eventually, closure.

You will see yourself in these letters. You will hear your own words. You may find yourself shouting out loud at what you're reading, "Yeah! That's what I'm talking about!" Or you might find yourself shedding a tear when you discover one of Rachael's letters tapping into a really personal space inside yourself.

We each bring our own lives to this book. These letters will mean something different to each of you who read it. What triggers me might not trigger you. Your personal life experiences will dictate your journey.

Keep your own journal or notebook handy to write some of your own letters along the way. You'll be surprised at how much you have to say!

In the end, it's all about **Girl Power**. Never forget that each and every one of you possesses that. And this book is key to tapping into that supersource!

With Love and Empowerment,

Lisa Goich

Author, *14 Days: A Mother, A Daughter, A Two-Week Goodbye*

Founder, *A Girl on the Go,*
www.AGirlOnTheGo.com

Introduction

An Opening Letter to My Readers

Dear Readers,

Thank you for picking up *Letters from a Better Me: How Becoming an Empowered Woman Transforms the World.* I know there are many books to choose from and mine is in front of you. Trust that feeling that this is the book for you right now. No matter what you read within these covers, remember that you were led here, and that must mean you are ready for big change. Don't let this intimidate you. You *are* empowered, even if you've forgotten.

How will reading this book help you transform the world? When we become truly empowered women, we are open to see clearly. We are not lost in the chaos and confusion of fear-based living and thinking. Once we learn to see ourselves, we see the power we have within us to transform how we interpret the world around us. When we do that, we begin to authentically represent what we stand for instead of putting our energy into what we fear or are against.

One of the most important parts about being the empowered woman is trusting our intuition. You will read things that will stir feelings up in more ways than you know what to do with. However, if you stick it out, I promise you'll come out feeling more empowered than you have before. You may even reach the point of a total transformation. It all depends on how deep you're willing to go.

You will have new tools to better yourself and the world around you. My words aren't new. Some of the most celebrated souls who ever lived have expressed the idea of bringing out the best version of ourselves. Sadly, those concepts have been buried in the rubble of all the anger, hatred, division, fear, and loss that have been flashing incessantly in front of us.

We start this journey lost in the throes of angry waves hitting the shore: harassment, rape, inequality, discrimination, oppression, and ego. We are exposed, breathless, and vulnerable, fighting for survival. Blinders off—we become *AWARE* of our own rage, anger, fear, and darkness. We are caterpillars working through the muck in order to transform.

Once our blinders are off, the angry energy of the waves subsides. We get the space to breathe as we move into *ACCEPTANCE* of the reality with which we are faced. We discover how to let go of what has already happened and brave our own fears to see who we are. We build our strength through acceptance, empathy, and compassion for ourselves and others. We begin to see how beating ourselves up is *not* productive. Self-abuse is *not* acceptable for the empowered woman. We sit in our chrysalises of self-reflection. We open our eyes to the unique, strong, passionate, smart, loving, beautiful, and amazing people we already are. The best version of ourselves comes to the surface.

In the last stage of our journey, we take *ACTION*— *becoming the empowered women who transform the world*. We are no longer fighting for survival. We've become one with the Ocean. We can do this because we became AWARE, ACCEPTED, and are now taking ACTION. By moving forward with love and compassion at our core, we bring the empowered woman's cause to listening ears. We bring her into our daily lives. We live the life of a true empowered woman. By doing this, we begin to transform the dark energy consuming our planet into an illuminating force driven by our own authentic color and light—the Butterfly.

If we act before we've become aware and accepted, our actions won't be as powerful or be done for the right reasons. Our ears are still closed. We attack a situation as if our way is the only right way, and others resist our message, which is built on the anger and fear plaguing our planet. We keep fighting against what we don't want. We feed the negative energy until what we do want is completely lost in translation.

You may notice that the book has three parts and nine chapters. This is by design. Three is one of the most powerful numbers in religion, spirituality, and transformation. It also represents the three As: AWARENESS, ACCEPTANCE, and ACTION. Nine represents the completion of divine will. These numbers have been brought to me during the most defining parts of my journey. They have represented some of the best endings and the greatest beginnings.

Throughout the book, I will be asking you to go deeper. These sections are exercises to help you get the most out of this journey. Do you have to do any of the exercises I suggest? NO! I know when I've read books in the past that told me to do something I didn't want to do, was too lazy to do, or made me scared of what I would see, I would put down the book and not pick it back up again. Then I would feel this shame from deep inside, eating at me, like I wasn't good enough. If you are laughing or shifting in your seat right now, you get where I'm coming from. These are all simply suggestions. If they feel right to you, do it! If they don't, leave it. Find the practice and pace that works best for you.

Are you intrigued? Get your notebooks, pull out your phones to loop in your trusted friends, and start really listening to your own letters coming out as you become A Better Me—*The empowered woman who has the power to transform the world—One loving action at a time.*

With Love, Compassion, and Hope,
Rachael Wolff

FOR BEST RESULTS: Pay close attention to the feelings that come up! Take notes about them in the margins. Use them to write your own letters and get as personal as you can. The letters here are not *all* a personal reflection of what I feel. They are meant to stir you up and trigger where you stand on different issues. They are used as a catalyst to uncover buried anger, judgment, fear, and rage, then open you up to shift, heal, grow, and expand. If you find there is not a letter that pertains to your exact situation, write it yourself.

WARNING: No matter what comes up for you on this journey, try not to judge yourself for having dark feelings. Just get them out, purge them. You need to see them before you can heal them. Believe me, they are coming out in some way. We are just getting real. We are on this journey because we are done with being in denial of what is happening in the world, and it all starts with seeing ourselves openly and with compassionate eyes.

BLINDERS OFF

'If the house is crooked and crumbling, and the land on which it sits uneven, is it possible to make anything lie straight?'[1]

— *Katherine Boo*

---

1   Katherine Boo, *Behind the Beautiful Forevers: Life, death, and Hope in a Mumbai Undercity* (New York: Random House, 2012), 250.

Chapter 1

ARE YOU KIDDING ME?

> ## FOR THE WOMEN WHO HAD THEIR BOUNDARIES CROSSED BY A MAN...

Dear Women,

Have you ever just disliked a guy? You don't appreciate anything he represents. He's the type to shove his politics in your face, degrade women, push alcohol, and act as though he should be on some kind of manly pedestal.

Well, I'd been uncomfortable around this one guy for a long time. I was only around him because his wife and I were friends. My stomach would tighten up anytime he came in the room. I can be friendly with most people, but there was something about the way he talked that triggered a visceral reaction in me. My fists involuntarily clenched.

I really tried to be friendly and see the best in this man. I honestly couldn't get in a conversation with him without feeling this rage build up inside me. I would ask questions, and he would dig himself in deeper. He didn't want to hear that what he was saying had no merit. I had to walk out of the room when he was talking on multiple occasions. Those times when he would get on the he-knows-everything pedestal, I would instantly have somewhere else to be.

At a gathering one night, after he had been obviously drinking way too much, he saw me and came over. I did my standard one-arm reserved hug, and he pulled me in to lick around my ear. I didn't know how to react beyond my incensed internal, ARE YOU FREAKING KIDDING ME? I would love to say I cold-cocked him, but my body froze.

I just tried to act as normal as I could and get away from him. I abruptly left the house. Why couldn't I at least call this man out? I left and went right to a friend's house, so disgusted by what had just happened.

At first, I didn't know if I should say anything about the incident to anybody. I went to a place of shame, like maybe I did something wrong. I found myself questioning my dress, my hug, and my overall presence. I can't tell you how many times I didn't say anything when a man made inappropriate comments or gestures toward me. I didn't want to embarrass them. Why am I worried about embarrassing them when they obviously have no regard for what I feel? They could give two shits if I'm triggered to relive a rape or former abuse. They aren't even seeing me as a fellow human being. In their eyes, I'm smaller than them. Rage fills me just thinking about all of them.

I would shake every time I thought of his tongue touching my face. I didn't know what to do. I did not ever want to be in the same room as that man again. I couldn't imagine having to listen to one more line coming from his disgusting mouth. I knew I was going to have to deal with it and talk to his wife, but I had no intention of speaking another word to him. I figured he would probably be too drunk to remember. If he didn't remember, it didn't happen, right? I've known way too many men who think that, just because they don't "remember," we, the victims, shouldn't feel violated. Ugh, I just threw up in my mouth.

Why are men so scared of women not being under their control? Wait, there I go again, writing "men," like it's ALL men. No, it's not all men. In fact, is it really about men at all? What the hell is going on? Why do some people feel so superior to others that it justifies hate language, sexual harassment, and not taking any responsibility for their actions?

A Disgusted Me

FOR WOMEN WHO HAVE PUT UP WITH UNACCEPTABLE BEHAVIOR...

Dear Whoever,

I just heard another story about a woman being treated like a lesser human being in the workplace. How are men getting away with this shit? How have we become so blinded that we keep letting these power-hungry men treat women like they are objects brought here for their amusement? Is this really happening? Why do we have to worry about being taken the wrong way by doing our jobs?

Does a man think that, just because he has a lot of power, he can do what he wants? All this takes me back to my early twenties, when powerful men tried to make me feel as though I had to sleep my way up the ladder if I wanted to get to the top. I remember feeling so alone while it was happening to me. I felt ashamed to tell anyone. I was made to think that somehow it was my fault that they made passes at me. "If I wasn't so..." Fill in the blank; I've heard it.

I'm physically hurting inside, hearing all these stories. I feel the rage festering in my stomach and burning through my limbs. This is not right! How could so many people turn a blind eye to this type of behavior? How have we made it okay and acceptable?

I can't believe this is still happening. How did we get here?

A Traumatized Me

ARE YOU KIDDING ME?

Our unguarded truthful reaction about the craziness we see in humanity

When we have that sort of thought, it's the call to awareness about what is really going on in our heads. All the anger, frustration, fear, and rage go on alert and make us question our beliefs about humanity itself. We go on judgmental rampages and spew harsh views to anyone who will listen, thinking we are standing up for our gender and making a statement. Fist raised, we fight against. "*Are you kidding me?*" translates to: *Watch out, world, you are about to feel my wrath.* Who knows what will arise from the depths?

Life has an interesting way of showing us how much progress we've made. When we have these kinds of "*I'm giving you a piece of my mind!*" reactions that make us question our own humanity, we still have a lot of work to do in our innermost depths. Why? It's an unconscious reaction. We show our rage and anger, but we won't show our peace and humanity. We are not going to make the best world-changing decisions in this space. Fighting *against* the problem won't solve the problem. When we react like this, we are ready for war. We are not at peace, because we aren't peaceful within ourselves. We haven't had a chance to question our own thoughts and beliefs, let alone consider the perspective of anyone we disagree with.

As women, we in some way have contributed to our lack of value in the world. We need to see the truth about where this anger is coming from.

- How are our feelings, thoughts, perspectives of truth, and actions affecting our reality?
- How are others affecting our inner and outer world?

Women are experiencing a lot of collective pain right now. Some may consider this a bad thing, but I see it as an *awakening*. It's women's *time to rise*. The flame has been lit. We are struggling to find our footing in this awakening of women's spirits. There needs to be a point where we transition from the victim role to #IKnowMyWorth. The time is now!

FOR WOMEN WHO HAVE FELT SLIGHTED BY OPPORTUNITIES AND PAY...

Dear Outraged Women,

How the hell did we get here? I'm infuriated at how judgmental companies can be just knowing the applicant is a woman. It's looking more and more like we need to do blind resumes, interviews, and testing to get out of our judgmental ways in the workplace. Why is pay different for a man versus a woman? Minority women are getting paid less than white women for the same jobs with the same qualifications. Resumes can be flagged based on the name at the top as *'read"* or *"don't read."*

This is absurd! Our racism and sexism show so much in the workplace.

Why is this happening? We need more feminine energy out there, no matter what nationality we are! How can a company see from all angles if it doesn't represent all angles in its hiring process? A company that can capture female and male strengths will have more to offer, but instead they just suppress the woman's voice by showing her she's not as appreciated, her education and experience doesn't matter, and that her strengths aren't as important as a man's. Do these companies think we can't be as productive as a man because we can/do bear children?

Some arguments are made that women aren't applying for the best jobs. Then the question is, *why* aren't they applying? Are they advertising in publications women read? Is their marketing aimed more toward men? What are they doing to support equal rights for women? When women do apply, there must be a way to ensure equal consideration and pay. We are not that stupid! Business owners need to rise up and come up with pay for a job, man or woman, minority or Caucasian, regardless. The pay is the pay!! It's not right that a woman has to prove herself so much more to close the gap in pay. My friend was just told she couldn't get a raise because she capped out, but a man doing the same job with fewer qualifications is making more than she is. How the hell could she be capped out if she is making less than a male at the same management level? THIS DRIVES ME CRAZY!! She won the company awards and he lost them some big customers, yeah, he fucking deserves to be paid more... WHAT THE HELL!

This is an outrage! I can't believe we are really still here! If I'm just as qualified to have the job, then I should have an equal opportunity to get it and to prosper in the same way as my male counterpart. The gaps are so ridiculous. How are companies and men still getting away with this?

An Outraged Me

FOR WOMEN WHO FEEL HOUSEHOLD EXPECTATIONS ARE WAY OFF...

Dear Household Partner,

I don't know who assigned the household rules, but I have some serious bones to pick. If two parents are working full-time, why, in many cases, are women still the ones expected to handle childcare, cooking, and cleaning? How the hell are we still here? Here, honey, you go have a drink and decompress in the living room while I do the homework with the kids, make dinner, and figure out how to get to baseball by six and dance by six thirty. But hey, you enjoy your relaxation time; you need it!

Oh wait, let me do the dishes after I make dinner. You go play with the kids or watch TV. Then give them to me when it's time for their baths and getting ready for bed. Wait, I still have the house to clean after your play session. Oh, you want another beer? Are we living in the era of the 1950s perfect-family stay-at-home-mom TV shows? Well, I'm not staying at home. I'm working too. There needs to be equal responsibilities in the household. If you are sitting around, it should be because we are *both* done doing everything we need to do and we get to relax together, or both enjoy our own time as individuals.

Oh, now that I've been going nonstop since five thirty this morning, you want to have sex. If you wanted sex, you should have cooked dinner while I helped with homework. Got the kids bathed and ready for bed while I did the dishes, since you made dinner. I don't have a partner, so I can be stuck doing everything. I chose having a partner because I thought we were in this together. I didn't want someone who was just going to sit and watch me do all the work and then say, "You didn't tell me you needed help." REALLY???

If you had that attitude at work, you would be fired. Give me a break! I'm so sick of being exhausted all the time. Sometimes I look at my friends who are single moms, and I wonder how much harder that really is, if I'm doing everything already. I didn't sign up for this. How can you not see that it's wrong for you to be relaxing if I'm still working to get the kids and you taken care of? How can you not see the picture enough to take the reins and do something to help? Make a fucking chart if you need to, but don't be sitting around doing your own personal stuff while I'm busting my ass. I want to relax and do personal stuff too.

A Fed-Up Me

HOW THE HELL DID WE GET HERE?

A question many of us have asked ourselves as we fall into our assigned submissive roles as women

It has been a long time since we gained the right to vote, but are we any closer to being viewed with equal value? Has there been progress? Yes, there has been. Have there been setbacks? Well, duh!

Sometimes we are blinded by roles that have been passed down from generation to generation as acceptable. We have done so much to advance, but we are still limiting ourselves when we can't see the worth of every individual. How are we going to get past color, race, sexual orientation, and religious belief if we can't even get to the balance between *his* and *her*, *yin* and *yang*? Are we ready to open our eyes enough to see that we aren't helping anyone by keeping someone else down? We don't have to be against anyone. We can simply be for humanity. We are not in a competition to be better than anyone else. Our purpose is to be the best version of ourselves. So, I repeat, *how the hell did we get here*?

- Where are these beliefs about being less-than coming from?
- Where are we accepting unacceptable behavior?
- Are we communicating our feelings, or putting our energy into more of what we don't want?

FOR WOMEN QUESTIONING FAITH...

Dear Spirit,

I don't even know who is listening when I write this. Is it God? Is it a great void in the Universe? If there is a Being up there or in me somewhere, tell me, how the hell did we get here? I don't even know what to call you anymore. I'm angry! I don't know how in some cultures women are revered, and in others we are feared and kept small. I don't get how people are still using religion as a tool against other people. Is that really what you want? Do you want people to feel more than or less than someone else? Am I supposed to love you or fear you? Am I supposed to love my neighbor or fear them? Am I supposed to love myself or not think of myself at all? It is so confusing. If I don't understand where you stand, how am I possibly supposed to understand how to treat myself and others? Everything seems to be for or against; love or fear. If I have so much confusion with you, how am I not supposed to be confused dealing with other humans?

I can't love and fear you at the same time. That is not peace. I can't feel peace inside me if I'm in a constant battle about what you represent in my life and how to honor you and my fellow humans. My internal battle starts with my not understanding you.

Spiritually Lost

FOR WOMEN WHO ARE ENRAGED BY OTHER WOMEN'S ACTIONS...

Dear Women-Bashing Women,

Now I feel like I have really seen it all. How do we expect men not to be against us when so many of us are against each other? You don't agree with my parenting style—don't do it! You don't agree with my hairstyle—don't get it done! You don't like my clothes—don't wear them! You don't like what my life looks like—don't choose to live like me! Even over all that, what really has me the most enraged is the women who are criticizing the brave women coming forward reporting abuse and harassment. ARE YOU FUCKING KIDDING ME? REALLY?!?!

Who are you to say anything to a woman that brave? You should be thanking her. She is contributing to stopping a cycle, so it stops getting passed down from generation to generation. Our daughters won't have to suffer as we did. Our daughters' daughters will suffer less than they did. Then, at some point, girls won't feel like they have to shut up and be quiet when a man tries to take advantage of them.

Just because you may have put up with it and it doesn't bother you, that doesn't mean that anyone who feels differently shouldn't voice it. I won't put up with any abuse so that you can feel comfortable. I'm done with women like you thinking you are representing the majority of women. You are for abuse if you can belittle a woman for coming forward. You are against women's rights.

I'm sorry if you put up with this from parents, boyfriends, and/or husbands, but REALLY, do you think other women should have to shut up and be silent? Is that really what you think? These women aren't whining. They finally have a place to raise their voices and say what they have been dying to say.

These are the women who would embrace you if you needed it, and you are turning your back on them. What are you hiding from? What is creating that dark wall inside you that can make you act so cruel? Do you really feel that little inside that you need to tear another woman down?

A Brave Woman's Friend

FOR THOSE WHO ARE FED UP WITH THE NEGATIVITY ON SOCIAL MEDIA...

Dear Social Media Users,

Really? I mean REALLY! I'm at the point where I can't stand social media anymore. We have spiritual beliefs and somehow, by practicing prayer, we are insulting others. If we are members of a minority and speak up, others may assume we are trying to represent our whole culture instead of just expressing our personal beliefs. Can't we have our own personal opinions without it turning into a war? Christianity can't agree on everything from church to church. Doctors don't always agree on how to treat people. A man can't be the voice of ALL men. A woman can't be the voice of ALL women. We are each individuals who accomplish great things and make mistakes. We sometimes say things out of ignorance. It doesn't mean we are sexist, racist, anti-gay, anti-religion, right-wing, left-wing, or anti-men.

Why are we so quick to judge instead of asking questions? If we see something we don't like, why do we have to attack before we find out what was really happening? Why do we like to judge people and situations so negatively so fast? Now, I'm not saying that, if someone makes a completely racist or sexist comment, we shouldn't call it out. And we do that by asking if that is what they meant and then educating them if they were just being ignorant.

But what I'm witnessing is that we are full of so much anger. I'm watching people spew out hate in responses to sometimes innocent or maybe ignorant people sharing a moment on social media. When did we become such a shaming society? Is that what social media brought us? Have we been being groomed for this? Are the haters really the majority?

A Terrified Me

ARE YOU UNCOMFORTABLE YET?

The question that will lead some to avoidance, denial, and addictions and others, who are ready to face all the darkness, to awareness, acceptance, and positive action

Here's where we need to be careful and often get stuck. A flame is ignited inside us by injustice. We're angry and frustrated and we want change. We react in our pain states. We make rash decisions, not considering the whole. We actually feed our negativity into honorable causes. People end up knowing what you are against, but not what you are for. This will continue as long as the message is driven by fear, anger, rage, and resentment. If what you are reading is making you squirm, good! Squirming is what the caterpillar does before it transforms into a butterfly. Now is the time to get uncomfortable. There has been an invisible barrier keeping women at a certain level. We are getting ready to shatter it. The question is: *Are you ready?*

This stage can be painful for women who have experienced trauma. It can also be painful for men who treated women as less-than without thinking anything of it. The role of villain may seem obvious, but some of these men are unconscious of what they are actually doing. When they are forced to open their eyes, the shame and guilt spiral can take them down. Whether a person is the perpetrator or the victim, some will use drugs, eat, drink, shop, gamble, and/or become relationship junkies, to name a few escape mechanisms. They will do these things so that they don't have to feel through the pain. During these painful times, we will question our spirituality and core beliefs. We can't pretend the questioning isn't there.

Some of women's biggest champions are men who have made horrible mistakes in devaluing women. Let's give people a chance to change before we attack. Some of the most vicious personal attacks on women come from other women who are caught in some sort of cycle of denial of their own truth. As we get stronger, we become clearer. Come on, part of being empowered women is trusting our instincts. Don't let rage cloud one of our greatest gifts.

I know it's uncomfortable, but it's important for our growth as conscious humans. We can't stay in the dark about where people are and where we are. This is a step in the transformation to becoming empowered women. Get in the dirt and FEEL through it. If we ever want to get healthy, we must process the deeply buried feelings first. When it comes to personal, communal, and environmental growth, we *must* get uncomfortable. When we get uncomfortable, we move and we shift. That is how we shatter the status quo.

STRUGGLE TO LOOK IN THE MIRROR...

Dear Me,

I hate you. Why are you so stupid? Why did you let him do this to you again? Why can't you stand up for yourself? Why are you such a doormat? You keep giving and giving and now you are empty. What else do you have? No one wants you. You can't do anything right.

You mess up everything! Look at you! Standing in the mirror, I see your cellulite, and your stomach jiggles more than Jell-O. How do you expect someone to even want to see you naked? People have no idea the person you really are. Okay, put on that fake smile again. Maybe they won't notice how you have to drink and eat yourself to sleep every night because you're so miserable.

You are always talking about your problems. You need to distract others from how pathetic your life is. You are constantly on defense. You hate your life. Life hates you. I hate feeling this way about you. I want to understand how you got here. Why do you keep attracting men who treat you horribly and women who backstab you? When did you stop being happy? Were you ever happy? How do I stop hating you?

A Broken Me

TIRED OF FEELING TRIGGERED...

Dear God,

I really don't like people anymore. I could once look at everyone with a neutral face. Back then, I didn't have a problem with what politician people sided with. I could even see their prejudices with compassion, because those came from the way they were raised. Lately, however, my compassion is wavering. I never thought that would happen. How did I get here?

I have worked so hard not to be against another person or group. I'm not perfect, but it has been a very long time since one person's character could trigger an internal rage so deep that it makes me want to step out and do something. I can't stand the person I'm becoming. I feel angry all the time, and the smallest altercation makes me want to scream my head off.

The problem is that I know without a shadow of doubt that what I fight against, I make stronger. I've heard this message over and over, starting with the famous quote by Mother Teresa: "I was once asked why I don't participate in anti-war demonstrations. I said that I will never do that, but as soon as you have a pro-peace rally, I'll be there." I don't know why some quotes stay with you for a lifetime, but that one has.

I never wanted to be against men, because I believe in the value of women. That is why what is happening now is really bothering me. I don't want to be against the voters who see value in another human being. I know that even in the chaos there is value. Yet, I still find myself here. I feel more and more prejudices seeping in. I don't want to live with so much anger inside me.

I don't want to go in to work feeling like I'm viewed as less than for being a woman. I don't want to judge men who have been recognized for their achievements. I don't want to feel like I must be polite when I've been violated. I don't want to feel the double standard of roles in relationships. I don't want to be filled with this angry energy all the time. God, Divine, Universe, Angels, Buddha, Jesus, Allah, Source, and/or Great Spirit, whatever name I need to call you to make this pain go away, please save me! Please show me the way to make the changes I want to see instead of focusing all my energy on what I don't want in my life. Please, heal the hate in my heart and show me a better way to live. Help me become a better me.

A Hopeful Me

WHAT DO I DO NOW?

What if there was a way for someone to guide you through the steps of becoming the best version of yourself? Okay, maybe it won't be easy, but I'm here, right here in the trenches with you. Let's really let the crud surface. It's there anyway, buried deep inside, destroying your foundation. We can't build a solid house if you aren't willing to fix your foundation. If you keep trying to build with a foundation full of rage, anger, fear, and hate, you will keep triggering explosions and destroying your progress. Let's work together to bring it up gently, and clean up your foundation so you can build something beautiful that will last. Here's where we begin:

Deep breaths. Fully breathe in to the count of five and exhale to the count of five. Do this three times. Take a second; sit with the emotions that are stirring inside you. Remember to fully exhale when you feel something triggering you. Don't hold your breath. This breathing practice gives us the space we need to open our minds to awareness of our own feelings, thoughts, and perspectives.

Drink a lot of water. You are cleansing a lot of toxic energy running through your body. If you drink a lot of water, it will help you stay physically and emotionally hydrated. This process can take a lot out of you. Think of it as cleaning your pathways. Visualize the water opening your heart as it runs through you.

Letter writing. Use the technique in this book to help you be honest and get out all your anger, fear, rage, frustration, gratitude, acceptance, and understanding of yourself and others.

- If you are judging other women, write about it!
- If you are bashing yourself, put it all on paper!
- If you are hating on men, scream it out!
- If you have underlying prejudices against others, preach it.

Get it out so you can see the darkness you're carrying around. You don't have to share these with anyone, but make sure you hold onto them for the duration of the book. The darkness lurking within is what you are projecting onto the world. The first step in healing it is seeing it. Take responsibility for what you are putting out there! Part I is about seeing what is going on inside honestly. Don't sugar-coat it!

Watch how the letters transform throughout the book and become more powerful and feed the empowered woman you are. I found this to be one of my biggest transformation tools. Letter writing changed my life and my relationships. Writing things in this form is like writing up a contract and signing it. I am committed to become a *better me*.

Journal. Write about anything that stirs you up while you're reading this book. It can be something in your daily life or in the book itself. Knowing what your triggers are is the first step toward taking back your power and becoming the empowered woman. If you don't know your triggers, you aren't in control of your feelings, thoughts, perspectives, actions, and reactions. Just keep writing. If a topic that makes you squirm isn't in here, write about it yourself. Get it out, get ugly, and get dirty. Most of all—get real. Be conscious of what you are putting out there. Part I is not for you to read and go out and spew your pain to the world. Part I is about taking off your blinders, reflecting, and getting real with your pain. When you think about the feelings and thoughts you are projecting, ask yourself:

- Is that really what you want?
- Are you in a place of love or fear right now?
- What feelings are coming up as you sit quietly?

Book buddy. Book buddies help you stay committed to the process. Read the book together and do the exercises. If you choose the book-buddy route, be careful whom you choose. You want someone whose goals for personal and spiritual growth are similar to yours. You will fuel each other. Are you fueling the light inside your heart, or is one of you wanting to burn things down and create more darkness? One route will create more love in the world, and the other will create more hate. You have to feel comfortable to be completely vulnerable with the person or people you partner with. You want someone who is on the journey to bring out her empowered woman too.

For the remainder of the book, you will be given the option to go deeper with a variety of exercises. These exercises are designed to help you to go as deep as you are willing to go. The deeper you go, the greater your transformation. This is your journey! Think of it as creating a garden. You will need to get the soil ready, pick and choose the seeds you want to plant, pull weeds, and nurture your garden to reach its greatest potential. You will get back what you put into it. You get to decide how amazing you want your garden to be. First you have to prepare the foundation and clean up the toxic muck lying beneath the surface. Are you ready?

Chapter 2

HOW DID WE GET HERE?

FOR WOMEN READY TO SEE OUR UNCONSCIOUSNESS...

Dear Self,

I don't remember driving to the store today. When I was in the store, I couldn't tell you how I ended up with the food I did. I don't remember picking broccoli over asparagus. He doesn't like broccoli. How did I do that? What is wrong with me? He is going to be so mad that I don't have a vegetable he likes. He's going to think I don't care. Do I need to go back to the store? I don't want to have another night like the last time I forgot to get mashed potatoes to have with our steaks. What if I just went to the liquor store and got him a bottle? Maybe he will notice my kind gesture, and the broccoli won't be a big deal.

Holy shit! When did I eat lunch? I'm not hungry, so I must have. What did I even have? What was I doing? Oh, that's when the kids' school called and told me about what's going on with the other kids at school. I'm so worried about my boy. He can't handle all the cruelty in school. How are these kids' parents okay with their children being such bullies? I wonder if they're bullies too. They probably are, or they just flat-out neglect their kids, so the kids are looking for attention. My son is so sweet and kind. Why does he have to go through this? Do I need to toughen him up? I used to be bullied. I never could understand why I was a target. I don't want him to go through what I did.

Oh no! It's already dinnertime. What am I going to do? Where did my day go?

A Frazzled Me

BEING UNCONSCIOUS

Many of us react to situations and people in our lives unconsciously. We have no idea when are being triggered by the past or when we are projecting fears of the unknown future. A broken record starts playing in our heads, and we go off about always, never, and our attachments to the unknown future. We have no idea that we are reacting to a past hurt or future fear. We aren't where our feet are. Our thoughts have taken us away to another place. Where our feet are becomes unconscious and the gifts of the present moment are lost. The potential for healing turns into expressed hurt, rage, anger, fear, and pain. The cycle of unconscious living continues. What is happening right now in the moment is what matters, but when we are unconscious—we miss it!

Autopilot is a great example of being unconscious. We don't want to deal with what is happening right now, so our minds go to past and future, and we miss what is happening. This is where our lives can slip out of control. We get lost. I can remember getting myself into a long-lasting emotionally abusive relationship. Next thing I knew, years had passed. When I was finally ready to look at the situation, I realized I had lost my identity completely. Looking back years later, my mom and sister told me, "You disappeared." My best friend from childhood said, "You were a robot." I was living unconsciously to avoid having to change, which in my mind meant I had failed. Discovering I had been living unconsciously was the beginning of my transformation.

Dear Friend,

I hate men! *All* men suck! *All* they want to do is use women for sex. We can be thrown away like trash. I'm so disgusted by *all* these men thinking they have the right do to whatever they want. They don't think there are any consequences. Especially *all* white men. White men think they are God's gift to humanity. It's even worse if they are rich white men. *All* rich people suck in general. They only get rich because money is *all* they care about. Then they think they can buy anybody. That's why *all* these powerful men think they can get away with everything. To rich people, money is power. Money sucks! I *hate* money! I never have enough money. I'm *always* going to be broke. I'm going to end up with some poor guy who beats me because I obviously don't deserve better. I'm *never* going to end up with a guy who cares about me. Men suck!

A Defeated Me

BELIEFS AND PERSPECTIVES

We are born and raised with a series of beliefs. Some were passed down from generation to generation. Others came from going with or against family, religious, societal and/or community beliefs. Some beliefs develop through our own personal experiences in school and life. Much of how we got to the reality we created is because of our beliefs, for better and for worse.

When we are lost in our fights against others, we haven't yet discovered that *our beliefs are perceptions*. As humans, we don't get to know absolutes like always, never, all, none, everyone, or no one. We are like snowflakes. Even within the same group, we are individuals. Beliefs vary from person to person within the same family, gender, religious group, workplace, support group, and culture. We can't all be right and someone else be all wrong. We each have our own unique view. Getting stuck in *I'm right* and *you're wrong* is how we block communication and close doors. We each have our own perspective of truth.

Pay attention to the perspectives that are creating fear and stress in your life. These beliefs will be shown in your reaction to others. We aren't reacting to a person in particular. We are reacting to our own beliefs or perspectives of thought about what the person represents. Any time we say *all*—all women, all men, all Christians, all Muslims, all single moms, all dads, or all Americans—we need to pay close attention. If we use the word *all* in that sense, there is a belief tied into it. See if the beliefs you hold are *really* true for you. By focusing on negatively charged beliefs, the negative (fear, anger, rage, hate, corruption, separation) is where our focus goes, and we create more of it.

If we are not clear in our perspective, we can get very confused and lose sight of the love within us. We can get so stuck in the perspective of fear that we forget what brought us to the relationship, situation, event, or cause in the first place. We submerge into the darkness of humanity.

DIG DEEPER

Belief exercise. Write about some of the beliefs that are a part of the foundation you build your house on. What do you believe? Remember to be honest! This exercise is to reveal hidden beliefs that could be causing us more pain. Here's a couple to get you going:

- Do I believe love hurts, or that hurt people are responsible for the hurt?

- Do I believe money (a piece of paper) is bad, or that it corrupts all who have it?

FOR THOSE OF US READY TO FACE OUR SHAME AND GUILT CYCLES...

Dear Universe,

I must be a truly horrible person. You keep knocking me down every time I start feeling good about a situation in my life. I have a great job and start to love what I do—I get laid off. I get into what I think is a great relationship—I find out he used me. I think someone is a great friend—she backstabs me. What did I do for you to punish me over and over? I really try to be a good person. If you loved me, you would give me the life I want. If you thought I deserved it, you would make good things happen in my life. I told my employer that if he valued me, he would let me work my own hours—he let me go. I told my boyfriend that if he loved me, he would marry me. Nope, he didn't love me. I told my friend that, if my friendship meant anything to her, she wouldn't be friends with this girl who doesn't like me. She's a friend to her anyway!

You keep bringing me so much pain. Am I really that worthless to you? Do I serve no purpose to you? I feel like if you really loved me I would be prettier. I wouldn't struggle with my weight and more people would want to be around me. I would be able to look in the mirror and be proud of who I am. I guess I'm just not worthy of being one of your beautiful creations. Maybe that's why you put me in a home where my brother was abused physically and I was abused emotionally. Maybe that's why I had to watch my mom being beaten. You didn't think I deserved more. I'm nothing.

A Broken Me

SHAME AND GUILT CYCLES

We may experience a horrific series of events: parental, sexual, physical, emotional, or mental abuse. Our parents, religions, teachers, and employers used to or could be still using shame and guilt techniques as a passive-aggressive way to get what they want. If we were children when these events happened, our undeveloped selves may have taken those shaming sessions in as part of our identity. If that happens, a shame cycle is initiated and the self-abuse begins. These abusive beliefs can go as far as making us think we don't deserve to breathe the air we're given. In our minds, we are bad people. Self-abuse can remain unconscious for a lifetime if it goes unchecked. How do you know if someone is abusing themselves? They are a negative force of fear in our world. It all begins with shame.

Shame creeps in, and our feeling of worthlessness starts feeding into our thought cycles. We are so ashamed of who we are that we create walls. This makes us easy targets for guilt trips. We don't feel worthy, so we need to do something for you whether it feels right or not. We can be convinced to stay quiet when bad things happen to us because we feel like we deserved it or somehow it was our own fault. We then will use the same cycle of shame and guilt to get what we want from others. The vicious cycle continues. We go on feeling like we are never good enough.

FOR WOMEN READY TO SEE HOW OUR LOW SELF-IMAGE HURTS US...

Dear Mirror,

I don't like the person you keep putting in front of me. Her eyes are too far apart. Her face is too round. Her hair is too stringy. Her skin is too pale. Don't even get me started on all the jiggling. How do you expect anyone to love her? What can I do to make her more acceptable? If I cover all her natural features, maybe she will be more lovable. If I get Spanks, maybe the jiggle won't disgust the people who have to see her. I can dye her hair to distract people from the roundness of her face. I take picture after picture of her, using all the editing features on my phone. I can make her more beautiful to the world. If at least fifty people don't like the picture, I didn't do a good job. I spend whole days thinking about how to make her look better.

I look into exercise programs, diets, makeup, and hair removal, yet no matter how many things I try, my attempt fails. I just can't look at you anymore, so I covered all the mirrors in my house. I don't want to think about what is in there anymore. I don't like what I see and I can't seem to change it.

I've just accepted that I'm not going to find anybody who will love the woman in the mirror. She's pathetic. She can't do anything right. She fails at everything. Who would want her?

A Pathetic Me

LOW SELF-IMAGE AND SELF-WORTH

This is how we got here, the land of misery. We believed we were unworthy and had to prove ourselves to the outside world. What we didn't realize is that we missed the messages that told us to *love ourselves first.* We missed the point where we might have been told *we only get more of what we already have inside.* We missed the vital importance of putting the *oxygen mask on ourselves first.* We just held onto being unworthy. If we feel unlovable, we try to get from the world what we aren't giving to ourselves. We expect the world to show us love.

We don't realize that we won't be able to spot it if we don't *first love ourselves.* We will attract people who will prove we are unworthy and unlovable. We will continue to attack ourselves, looking for any external way to make ourselves lovable— relationships, clothes, makeup, body alterations, and material goods—yet we will also get lost in addictions to food, alcohol, or drugs in order to continue our belief that we are unlovable. We beat ourselves up for our cellulite, shape, hair, and overall look. Then we tell the mirror that's why we aren't lovable.

A healthy person can look in the mirror and make changes too, but the difference is that they aren't doing it to seek outside worth. They aren't attached to what doing it means for someone else. They may be doing it as way to treat themselves. It's important to know the difference. When we are feeding a negative self-image, we are creating the darkness within us. Then we aim our darkness at something outside of us to lessen the pain.

As we become more and more aware of the negative cycles and our own unstable foundations, we will get the tools to create lasting change. We can't get there by building on the same unstable foundations (our negative self-image, self-worth, and self-respect), no matter how pretty we make our house and garden (how we make our outsides look). The house will eventually break down if it's not on solid and healthy ground. The only thing that's solid is *love*. A healthy relationship with ourselves has to come first. All other relationships take our lead, including our relationships with our spiritual lives.

FOR THE BRAVE WOMEN READY TO LOOK AT HOW UNPRODUCTIVE BLAME IS...

Dear Mom and Dad,

How could you do this to me? This is your fault. If you hadn't treated me like I couldn't make it, I wouldn't be a total failure. You *never* treated me like I could do anything right. You were *always* correcting me, and now I'm so scared of doing something wrong, I just freeze and need to be told exactly what do in order to feel like I'm not going to be fired. Despite this, I keep getting fired.

If you two would have just let me take some chances, I might not be the way I am today. Seeing you two fighting all the time has made me want to avoid all confrontations. I can't have a successful relationship to save my life. Do you two even love each other? It seems like you both have to drink just to put up with each other. You set an awful example for me. I'm scared of men because of the relationship you two have.

Why couldn't you two have just been normal? Why couldn't you be loving parents who encouraged me to go out there and do my best? Instead, you made me feel like I was a failure if I got anything less than a B. I couldn't be good enough for you, no matter what I did. Ugh, I wish I had had better parents, because if I had, I would be on *Oprah* right now sharing my successes.

A Disappointed Me

BLAME

If this letter puts you into a spree of blaming all the people who wronged you, you have a front-row seat to how you got here. Becoming aware of where we point fingers and blame is the first step to breaking the cycle. We need to approach it by looking back with different eyes. Our first response may be to blame someone else, a situation, or ourselves, and many of us have been taught that this is natural. "Mommy, Michael hit me." *I won't tell her that I threw a toy at his head first.* Blaming has become a part of everyday politics, religion, friendships, intimate relationships, family dynamics, and overall life. The people we hurt most with blame are ourselves. When we hurt ourselves, even if it is unintentional, we will hurt others. We project the negative energy we carry inside.

- How do you feel when you are blaming someone else?
- Does it make you feel good?
- Does it feel like you are getting any closer to a solution by blaming them?

When we are stuck in a blame cycle, we are also stuck in a victim cycle. This is not to say we are never victims of unacceptable behavior, but the question is: are we choosing to live in *victim mentality*? Victim mentality is different than being a victim of actions taken against us. With victim mentality, we become victims of the world and everyone in it, including ourselves. We don't look at our feelings, thoughts, and actions and how they contribute to the reality we are choosing to live in. When we keep the focus on us, we respond to negative situations in a healthier fashion. We stop pointing fingers and start coming up with solutions. When we question blame by asking what we learned from the experience, we shift the power from fear to love. How we got here was a lesson, nothing more, and nothing less. When we focus on blame, we haven't learned the lesson. We are destined to repeat the lesson until we learn it, or die miserable.

This is not an invitation to self-blame. Self-blame is different from taking responsibility for our feelings, perspectives, and actions. Self-blame involves an abusive element. Self-blame is more destructive than blaming others. Taking personal responsibility shouldn't turn into convincing yourself how much you suck. When we take personal responsibility for our part, we tell the Universe we are open to learning from experience.

LOOKING AT OUR FEARS...

Dear God,

I'm a God-fearing woman. I serve you by serving my family, the less fortunate, and my church community. I live the life I'm told is acceptable to live. When I fail, I come and confess my failings. I know I'm not worthy of the sacrifice Jesus made on the cross. I do try to prove to you that I'm worthy of walking this Earth. I do and do and do for others, but God, I'm so tired. I don't know what else I have to give. I keep feeling that, no matter what I do, it's never enough to satisfy you and get me to Heaven. I'm afraid of facing you and hearing that I could have done more. I fear you will send me to the Devil for all my human failings.

A Fearful Me

Dear Partner,

I'm so scared you are going to leave me. One day you are going to figure out I'm not worthy of your love and you are going to find someone better out there. I feel like, if I'm not with you every second, you are going to find someone else. When you go out with your friends, I'm petrified you aren't going to come back. Why are you even with me?

A Petrified Me

Dear Boss,

I really want to make you happy. You made an advance at me and I accepted because I really want to keep my job. I love this firm and I don't want to go out and have to look for another job. I don't feel comfortable with what happened, and I don't feel good about myself for not speaking up. I'm so scared of losing my job. What if no one out there thinks I'm good enough? If I make you happy, will I be good enough for you to look at what I can do? I'm scared the answer is that now you will only see me as a piece of meat. I'm scared that all the work I've done to get where I am will mean nothing. How do I get you to see my worth?

A Concerned Me

FEAR

Some of us have been living in fear as far back as we can remember. We feared what our fathers would do. We feared disappointing our mothers. We were taught to fear while learning new things. We were taught to fear the unknown, fear nature, fear people, and fear ourselves.

Many of us have been taught from a very young age to fear God (however you define the Creator). *"I'm a God-fearing woman!"* If as far back as we can remember we fear the one Being who is supposed to be the definition of love, how are we NOT supposed to live in fear of everything that comes our way? Fear keeps us all separate.

When we fear not being good enough, we do things to gain worth. We wonder why we fight to feel connected to the Divine. To fully connect to Source is a connection of love. If we are connecting to life through fear, we project fear. All the rage, anger, and hate stem from fear. If we fight for our own worth, we are fighting to see the worth in others. We judge, hate, and stand against someone else to distract us from looking at the very core of who we are, in fear of being unworthy and unlovable. Fear holds us back from seeing love.

DIG DEEPER

Investigate your fears. Write your fears down so that you can look at them on paper. Question your perspectives to see if your fears are keeping you from attracting the life you want to be living.

- How many times have you blocked love, peace, joy, and tranquility out of fear?

- Did you not go somewhere?

- Did you not take a job?

- Did you not move?

- Did you sabotage a relationship?

- Did you stop someone you love from doing what would make them happy?

- Did you miss an opportunity to connect with a person because you had different political or religious beliefs?

- Did you judge someone for the color of their skin or the church they go to?

- Where has fear taken over in your life?

TRAPPED BY ATTACHMENTS TO TITLES...

Dear Self.

I'm failing as a mom. No matter how hard I try, I can't get my kids to eat their vegetables. I can't stand all the fighting over the table. I've tried serving them in so many different ways and they still won't eat them. How am I going to make sure they do the right things in life? Other parents are going to look at me and not want to associate with me, the single mom who can't even feed her kids the right way. My kids are going to be so weak because I'm a failure at being a mom. I'm a horrible mom, and I'm destroying my kids.

A Failing Me

Dear Husband.

I keep trying to be a good wife. I have dinner on the table for you at six—no matter how many things I have to shuffle to do it. I do your laundry and hang up your clothes the way you like them. I sit and listen to you for hours on the porch as you go on and on about your day. I clean the house even though I absolutely hate cleaning the way you like it. I put aside my life for the sake of yours. When will I ever do enough for you to realize how lucky you are to have me?

An Overwhelmed Me

Dear Student and Parents of Students,

When I'm in the classroom, I do my best to get you all the information I'm required to give you. Then I try to make sure I see each of you as individuals. I go home and have stacks of paperwork and calls to make in order to be considered a good teacher. I really want to be considered a good teacher. I'm expected to take my weekends away from my family to serve you. Otherwise, I'm not a good teacher. Am I not supposed to have any life because I want to be a good teacher? I'm miserable in my personal life and my kids are suffering because I don't have time to be a good mom. Isn't that just as important as being a teacher? I'm so tired. I'm starting to fail at both. I don't know what to do. I want to be a good teacher. I want to be a good mother.

A Struggling Me

ATTACHMENT TO TITLES AND WORDS

Thoughts of being unlovable and unworthy can plague us. We start seeking our worth in what we do for others. The cycle of losing our identity in the titles and words begins. Now, it is about being a good daughter, friend, sibling, employee, boss, wife, mother, and spiritual follower. We are lost in a feeling of lack. We don't think we are worthy of being who we are, so we try to fill ourselves with the titles that make us worthy. We don't realize that, if we don't feel worthy just being ourselves, no title will ever make us feel worthy. We will use our failures as a source of more self-abuse. Then we'll start turning our definitions of the titles onto others, expecting them to live up to our attachments to those titles.

That's when we start reacting to the words that come with our own personal definitions. Let's use the word *bitch* as an example. The definition of bitch is female dog. Some women have embraced the word bitch to mean powerhouse and feel proud to be called one. Other women will take it as an insult. Our attachment to words makes it hard for others to navigate their way through our psyches.

Our attachment to our titles and definitions make us feel like righteous judges against ourselves and others. If you're letting a child play more than thirty minutes of video games, you're a bad mother. If you don't use the word God to describe your Higher Power, you're a bad person. If you don't come in early and leave late, you're a bad boss. We judge ourselves and others on a series of titles. We make ourselves righteous even if we are secretly self-abusing because we don't feel like we live up to the titles ourselves.

Become aware of your attachment to titles. See how you judge yourself and others based on titles. Christians, Muslims, Jews, man, woman, rich, poor, and on we go. Your relationship with and attachment to these titles could be causing you to manifest a reality you don't want. If we have a negative attachment to rich people, we will keep ourselves from becoming rich, because we are actually fighting against them in our minds. We will sabotage any money that comes into our lives to keep us at a level in which we feel worthy. It's not money or rich people that are bad, but our thoughts and feelings about them make them bad for us. We will even attract cruel rich people into our lives to prove our point. We get what we focus on. Be clear on what titles you are attaching to and how. If a title makes someone more or less, there is an underlying fear that needs to be faced.

DIG DEEPER

Uncover your attachment to titles. Make a list of as many titles you can think of that you use to define yourself or that others use to define you. Define each title. If a title serves fear, look at it and see how you can make it serve love instead. You are making observations. No one is asking you to change. Become aware of the choice and the possibilities. Now make lists of how you judge others according to those or different titles.

HOW WE CHOOSE TO SEPARATE...

Dear Women,

All men are the enemy. They want to keep us down. We have to keep them from getting into positions of power that will destroy us. We have to fight against them to stop this madness. We are at war. Women will win. We need to take over in order to correct all the messes they have made. They will feel my wrath. I'm not going to compromise. I'm not going to listen to the lies they keep spreading. Everything that comes out of their mouths is corrupt. I will take down this boys' club. I'm done with this shit.

A Determined Me

Dear Cannabis Supporters,

Are you kidding me? I don't know how you can think that cannabis being legal is good idea. Do we just want a bunch of potheads lying around? If people can grow it freely, we are going to have a bunch of lethargic hippies on our hands. I don't care what the research says. The research is bullshit. Even if it's used for medical purposes, I don't want it on our streets. This is the war on drugs. If you can't handle it, you should be behind bars.

An Anti-Drug Advocate

SEPARATION

Separation is making it *us* *against them*:

- Are we for women and against men?

- Are we for Caucasians and against other colors of skin?

- Are we for Christianity and against any other religious practice?

- Are we for peace and against war?

- Are we for creativity in the classroom and against standardized testing?

- Are we for legalized drugs and against illegal drugs?

You may be seeing some of these and wonder how it is disruptive to be against prejudice, war, standardized testing, and illegal drugs when we know these things have negative effects. *Against-them* thinking keeps us trying to fight prejudice with more prejudice, war with more war. You also may think about how research is finding that some illegal drugs are actually beneficial to have around. The point here is to become aware.

If we put our energy into what we are against, we separate from the changes we want to see. We may miss the benefits of what the other side has to offer. There may be a compromise that benefits the world, but, if our minds are closed, we won't be able to see it. If we don't act inclusively, we close our minds to different ways, to greater possibilities. We become righteous, and righteousness (which comes from fear) causes a war within. If we are at war within, how can we create peace?

With separation, we build walls internally and externally. Someone with a different perspective will stop listening if they feel like they are being yelled at like a child. Communication is shut down. We stop asking questions and start making statements. We carry conversations in our heads with people we won't even talk to, fighting against their ideas and values. The record of constant injustice playing in our heads creates a chaotic place to be. It's another way we give fear power over our lives. For now, watch and observe. By the end of the book, some of these separations will dissipate. They won't have the emotional attachment they once did.

Negative energy creates separation for the long term. Negativity is not empowerment. If there is separation, we are not operating in what is best for humanity. Division and fear are how we got here. We can't break the cycle by using the same tools that got us here in the first place. Isn't that the definition of insanity?

THE PROBLEM WITH PEDESTALS...

Dear Mom,

You are so perfect. I want to be just like you. I don't know how you do all the things you do. You are superhuman. You managed to get us all fed, do the laundry, work, and clean the house, and I never heard you complain. I feel like a failure as I try to balance life with my kids. You made it look so easy. You were always busy. I'm not sure I ever saw you stop.

I remember Dad would take us to the park and, by the time we got home, everything was immaculate. Even our snacks were organized. I was at the park with my kids the other day and then was so tired I went to sleep with my house a mess. How am I your daughter?

Your Imperfect Daughter

PEDESTALS

We start early and put our parents on pedestals. They are our first superheroes. We expect them to be better because they are our parents. Then we graduate to characters in fairytales. We get ideas of what love should look like. We see movies where princes rescue women. In our heads, it may translate to, if a man loves me, he will always show up in the nick of time. Then we start putting romantic partners on pedestals and, when they don't show up to rescue us, boom! Off the pedestal they fall. As an adult, we can want the romantic relationships we see in the movies, along with the happily-ever-after. When our focus is there, we don't even see the person in front of us because we are looking at them as a character we want them to be.

As adults, we put other people on pedestals, such as friends, teachers, professors, bosses, romantic partners, our children, politicians, athletes, and celebrities. They are superhuman. They have no right to make mistakes or do something we don't approve of; if they do, we let them fall with a thump off their pedestals and lash out against them.

Pedestals are a dangerous place, and no human belongs on them. We are here to learn. If we put people on pedestals, we judge them under unfair standards. We don't see them as like us; we see them as separate. When they are separate, we can easily go from being for them to being against them. We create a war.

HOW WE CONTRIBUTE TO THE PROCESS OF GOSSIP BECOMING NEWS...

Dear Friends,

Can you believe Cindy is leaving her husband? I heard she told him she was tired of him sitting around and doing nothing and she was leaving to go explore the country. She's so selfish. I don't know how she could just leave him. He is so nice. He is always so friendly to everyone. I don't think we should talk to her. I think we should stand by him. Who wants to bring him dinner this week?

A Concerned Friend

Dear Church Members,

I know we aren't supposed to be gossiping, but did you hear Meg and Dave's son is gay? He just came out to them. I don't know what they are going to do. I heard that they caught him in his room with another boy. I don't know what kind of parents they are to let something like this happen under their own roof.

A Saint

Dear News,

I'm tired of seeing all the he said, she said on the news. I don't know why you think I want to hear about this kind of gossip. What are the facts? I keep watching and all it does is stir me up. It's your fault we focus on gossip instead of facts. How could you do this? I'm disgusted by what news has become.

A Disturbed Viewer

GOSSIP, ENTERTAINMENT, AND NEWS

We created media today to be what it is. It started with us feeding the gossip cycle. Media just followed suit. They have to do what sells, or it wouldn't be successful. Then, as media sources expanded, we started to put our celebrities on pedestals. There were teen magazines that supported the gossip mills. We kept gossiping, and the media and news needed to keep up. They want to succeed; that's business. They have to go where the demand is. Politics showed us what we wanted by creating smear campaigns. Now, in hindsight, we may be realizing it is all too much when we struggle to find an accurate news source and are overwhelmed with all the drama in the world.

We can attach to the idea of entertainment sources keeping us in the darkness of humanity. They become our addictions, feeding our unworthiness. They reinforce how undeserving humanity is. You don't think you look good enough, cover up your imperfections, wear this not that, believe this diet will work, get rid of the circles, and strive for perfection. For me, it got so bad, I noticed how my life was mimicking what I was watching—my *thoughts* about what I was watching. One time, I even thought some guy who was throwing dog poop in a dumpster was disposing of a murder weapon!

Attaching to gossip, entertainment, and news takes us out of our own journey. How we take in what we hear and watch feeds the darkness or the light within us. We have to pay attention to where we are focusing our energy.

You and I could watch the same show and pull completely different things from it. It all depends on where our awareness lies and how in tune we are with ourselves. I can watch television through eyes of love, compassion, and empathy and see completely different messages than a person who watches the show with fear, judgment, and intolerance. I can sit and judge people for their mistakes, or I can celebrate the lessons and/or the heroes of the story. When I see love in any form, it may bring me to tears of joy. Someone else may focus on the circle of drama or the beliefs that aren't in line with their own. When you're listening to people or watching something, pay attention to where your thoughts are going. Is your energy contributing to what you want it to?

HERE'S A BIG PILE OF JUDGMENT...

Dear Everyone,

I feel like I'm constantly being judged. Stop judging me. You aren't better than me. You don't know what I've been through. You don't know what I've survived. Do you want to know why I'm an addict? It is because of you (blame). You, living your perfect little lives, I can't live up to that. I'm in a constant struggle (low self-image). You can preach whatever religion you want to me. I know what is right. You are all going to hell for judging me. You are all (separation) a bunch of hypocrites sitting on your judgmental stands (pedestals).

I'm sorry I'm not the perfect daughter (attachment to titles). I can't live up to the standards I obviously should be. Are *you* freaking perfect? I know you mess up. I hear about you all in your messed-up relationship bitching (gossip).

I'm sorry I'm so unlovable (shame cycle). Christians are so judgmental (belief). Really, all of you are the ones who need to be judged. I'm sorry I didn't follow Jesus the way you thought I should. He abandoned me (belief). How could God introduce me to those people who gave me the drugs? He was punishing me.

I watch these reality shows on TV and I don't get why these people get picked for this stuff (entertainment). I belong on TV. My story is more entertaining than any of theirs. If they want to see some real shit, they need to look at my life. I'm made for reality shows. Then maybe you would see me as more worthy of being in your space.

Maybe I am going to hell (fear). I watch people on social media (entertainment) and the news constantly judging people like me (news). Maybe the truth is I am worthless. I should be able to stop taking these pills. I should be able to stop drinking. I can't (belief), so I guess that makes me a piece of shit. I should be able to get my life together. My life would have looked so different if I didn't grow up the way I did. I might have even managed to be a better mom (attachment to titles). Maybe, if people reached out to help me instead of constantly judging me, I could have been this person you all think I should be.

A Distraught Me

JUDGMENT

All of the concepts above are tied into *judgment* of ourselves and *judgment* of others. Judging comes from us being *unconscious* of what we are really feeling inside. Our beliefs create a feeling of righteousness, and we start the judgments of *I'm right* and *you're wrong*. An internal *shame cycle* is manifested into judgment, which supports us using *guilt* tactics as we sit and judge. Our *low self-image* makes us want to take others down with us, tricking us into believing that it will make us feel better about our imperfections. We use *blame* as a source of judgment to avoid taking personal responsibility and doing something about what we are seeing—whether it is something inside of us or something in the world around us. *Fear* takes over, and we feed our fear with our own internal judgments, which in turn feeds what we put out in the world. We use our *attachment to titles* to judge ourselves and others as more or less than what they *should* be. Every time we judge, we create more *separation* from ourselves, our Creator, our community, and our world. We use *pedestals* to judge ourselves against someone else to support unworthiness. When the people we put on the *pedestals* fall, we judge them even more harshly. Finally, our internal judgments turn into external *gossip*. Our attachment to *gossip* taught the *entertainment* industry how to keep our attention. *News* became less about reporting facts and more about the choices to negatively judge whomever the masses want to be judging.

We will, however, never judge anyone worse than we judge ourselves. And the more negatively we judge ourselves, the more negatively we judge others. Keep self-judgment in mind when you hear someone else or yourself judging. Now, does this mean we are going to throw judgment to the wind and just stop judging? I'm laughing at even the thought of that possibly being realistic. We are judgmental creatures. We are going to make judgments and we are going to be judged by others. The key is to be conscious of our judgments and how we are receiving judgments from others. If we are reacting to someone else's judgment, it's because it is triggering a self-judgment within us. A loved one says, "She gained some weight." If we feel fat, we can have an off-the-rocker reaction and go off on the loved one, maybe because we feel like we've gained some weight and we are beating ourselves up about it. It is possible that the loved one was making a simple observation. They might have even thought the weight looked good on the person they were talking about, but if we just react, without pausing and asking questions, and judge them for what goes through our heads, we are reacting because of self-judgment. Seeing all this begins with awareness. Really tap into where the judgment is coming from. Is it coming from a fearful place or from a loving place?

DIG DEEPER

Make lists. Get ten pieces of paper. On the top of each sheet of paper, write the name of one of the concepts that was covered in this chapter. Under each title, write about how you have fallen into using this concept and how it made or makes you feel when you are participating in it.

Chapter 3

WHAT IS MY RELATIONSHIP WITH THE WOMAN IN THE MIRROR?

ATTACHING TO FAIRYTALES...

Dear Dysfunctional Family,

What is wrong with you people? Mom, I'm sick of you acting like Dad is doing something wrong for being a man, sitting around, having a couple drinks, going out to his man cave, and playing the father role. You have no grace for accepting your position as Mom. Dad is the provider. Your job is to do all the inside work. Dad, I don't get it, why are you yelling? Good dads never yell. Don't you know you are the one who needs to remain cool and calm at all times? Now, sisters and brother, you really have to be kidding me. You guys are all just a bunch of selfish assholes. What happened to ALWAYS being there to support one another and only saying kind things? What happened to, *if we don't have anything good to say, don't say anything at all*? OMG, our family is so messed-up. I can't stand to be around any of you. If I had a better family, I would like me more. I can't stand me! I'm not good at being a daughter or a sister. What is wrong with me?

A Pissed-Off Me

Dear Prince Charming,

Where the hell are you? I keep getting frogs. When are you coming to sweep me off my feet? I know you're out there! We are going to have the perfect life together as soon as I find you. I will finally get my happily-ever-after.

Are you not coming because I don't deserve to have a prince? Why don't I deserve to find you? What is wrong with me? Am I not pretty enough? What else do I have to do to get you to love me?

An Impatient Me

CLINGING TO A FAIRYTALE

Mirror, mirror in the bathroom, who do you see when you look at me? The fairytales: I would be happy if I had the perfect family. I would be happy if I had the perfect relationship. I would be happy if I looked like the model in the magazine. When we start believing we aren't enough (incomplete) being who we are, we define ourselves by unrealistic images. Anytime you hear yourself saying, *I would be happy if...*, there is a problem.

When we attach to fairytales, whether it is at home, in our personal relationships, careers, causes, financial life, spiritual life, physical bodies, or emotional bodies, we aren't being present. We are judging ourselves against someone or something that is not real. We are attached to a fantasy in the unknown future. If we are caught up in *images* of people, instead of seeing the people themselves, we are trapped in the illicit fairytale. Attaching to the fairytale will come back around and hit us where it really hurts: our self-worth, self-esteem, self-image, and self-awareness. Chasing happily-ever-after steals from our authentic joy and destroys any life we want to create.

Instead of seeing blessings and gratitude, we see lack. We focus our attention on what we don't have. We get angry with people in our lives for not playing the perfect fairytale roles. We put undue expectations on all the people involved to live up to characters written for the screen. The fairytale life blinds us from seeing the truth. Have you ever heard the saying *love is blind?* That is not my experience at all, but I do believe lust, infatuation, codependency, and attachments to the future make us blind.

We start getting mad at men, women, and children for not being our perfect fairytale characters. We are so smitten by the thought of happily-ever-after that we forget to look at happily ever NOW—the only place authentic joy exists is NOW.

DIG DEEPER

Attaching to Fairytale exercise. Now is the time to start paying attention to any of the times you are attaching to fairytales. Investigate all your *I'd be happy if* thinking and write it down so that you can review it. How is this thinking serving you to live your best life?

THE WOMAN IN THE MIRROR...

Dear Self,

Look at you. Do you really think you look good enough to pull off that shirt?

Look at the flab. I can see a muffin over those jeans. Nothing fits right. When did you get this fat? Nobody is going to love you. I don't know how you expect to be heard when you present yourself like this. I can't even stand to look at you. How do you expect people to respect you?

Okay, I need to get out of my head. It doesn't matter how I look. Nobody is looking at me anyway. Being invisible is why I always get passed over, whether it's in relationships or in my career. I just have to keep working hard and hopefully one day someone will see my value.

I don't understand why people don't value me. Maybe I really am unlovable. I'm never going to have the life I want, so I need to get my head out of the clouds and just face the fact that I'm stuck with myself.

I keep messing up! Maybe I have been with the right guy and I just fucked it up because fucking up is what I do. I screw up everything good that comes along. I'm such a dumbass. I wouldn't know something good if it hit me in the face. If I do see something good, I can't get it because I do something stupid to mess it up. Dear Self, I'm going to be alone with you forever. How pathetic is that? Miserable forever.

A Depressed Me

JUDGING THE WOMAN IN THE MIRROR

We can be very judgmental creatures, and the person we are hardest on is the woman in the mirror. She is the catalyst for all the love and fear we give to the world. Take that in! We can't hide from the way we really feel about the woman looking back at us. Even if we choose not to look at her, we will still project her out to the world. Our views of ourselves can become crystal clear when we sit in awareness while looking in the mirror. All our self-judgment is right there staring back at us.

The mirror tells us everything we think we are NOT and everything we think we ARE. This can be a VERY good thing if we choose to become our own best friend and hero, but it can have devastating effects if we choose to be the villain and enemy. Self-abuse leads to accepting abuse from others, whether verbal, emotional, mental, or physical. We accept unacceptable behavior when we can go back to that mirror and mentally and emotionally abuse the woman standing in front of us.

You are not alone!!! None of us are alone. We are here on this journey together, and the more we can bring our inner darkness to light, the more opportunities we have to heal it. Give yourself permission to cry. Allow your tears to heal your soul. You've been carrying all this weight and now, as you face it, the pain will subside.

No drug, amount of alcohol, shopping, eating, exercising, or simply avoiding will help heal you. You have to feel through this and face the woman in the mirror. This is not the place for blame, shame, guilt, or more self-abuse; that's what we do when we are feeding addictions to cover our pain. By becoming aware, you have taken a giant step. You are no longer living in the dark. We have to see what is going on inside if we are to stand any chance of healing anything on the outside.

DIG DEEPER

Looking in the mirror. Ask yourself:

- How do you feel about the mere image of yourself?
- Are you beating yourself up?
- Are you telling yourself you're not good enough?
- Are you looking at your face and body through eyes of love or fear?
- Are you focusing on features you like or don't like?
- What messages are playing as you look at yourself?
- Are these thoughts and beliefs serving you to be the best version of yourself?
- How do you feel about yourself for making a mistake?
- Are you calling yourself names when you don't meet others' expectations of you?
- What names are you calling yourself?
- Are you replaying a mistake over and over in your head?
- Are you quick to forgive yourself, or do you hold a grudge?
- Do you inflict physical and/or emotional pain on yourself?
- Why do you think you deserve this kind of treatment?
- Do you feel like you have value even when you make unhealthy choices?

FINDING HAPPINESS IN OUTSIDE FIXES...

Dear Happiness,

Are you a fantasy? I can't find you anywhere! I keep looking and searching. I try to look the way happy women do, but all I do is spend too much money on clothes, makeup, and plastic surgery. I thought I would find you in the gym. It just made me feel worse about myself every time I watched some guy talking to someone else and ignoring me as though I have some kind of disease. I tried to find you in books, but all they did was make me feel like I wasn't doing enough. I can't find someplace I belong. I don't quite fit in anywhere, and all my trying is just making me more miserable. I'm starting to believe I'm never going to find you. If I can't find you, does that mean I don't deserve you?

A Miserable Me

USING OUTSIDE FIXES TO FIX INSIDE PROBLEMS

Most of us have been taught that something outside of ourselves will fix the problems inside of us. Now, I know how perception can play tricks on us here. This doesn't mean that seeking help is a bad thing. We are simply becoming aware of how we unconsciously look to the outside to fix the inside.

We start getting programmed for this early. If you wear *this*, if you look like *this*, if you buy *this*, if you have *this* relationship, and if you go *here*, your life will magically be transformed. No product, person, or place is capable of filling in the missing piece within us. Only self-love can do that. When we try to seek transformation from the outside, we find more opportunities to go deeper into the abyss of depression.

Some of us fight for the "perfect body" our whole lives. We buy the exercise gadgets we use just a few times, and eventually we have a pile of equipment sitting in our closets collecting dust. We try this diet and that diet. We go to this gym and that gym. We constantly work to arrive at a body that we think will make us happy.

We can't possibly hear what our bodies are trying to tell us if we are constantly at war with them. What we have yet to realize is that, if we are at war with our bodies, we are actually resisting the results we are trying to achieve. We have to dig deeper. What do you think having the perfect body will change in your life? Some might say things like: I will be happier. I will be more confident. I will become more social. I will live better. I will attract men/women. I will be listened to. I won't beat myself up. The list goes on and on. You can have all those things no matter what your body looks like. The perfect body on the outside doesn't create peace on the inside. If we don't heal the inside, we will keep fighting. When we are at peace with ourselves, we are at peace with our bodies. We know our body is serving its purpose. We start exercising because we like feeling healthy. We eat because it feels good in our bodies. We are conscious of what we are doing because it feels better. When our insides are aligned with the results we want, we are at peace. Results come by doing the work and loving it.

TRYING TO FIND OUR WORTH IN DOING...

Dear Spirit,

I'm so tired. I've volunteered as much as I could. I keep a clean house as best I can, even though I feel like I never get to sit down. I work as many hours as I can squeeze into the day. I do all my family's laundry and get towels folded and put away. I cook balanced meals. I put my kids to bed at a reasonable hour. I do and do and do, yet I still feel like I'm not enough. I'm resentful and angry for all I'm doing. Is this why I'm not worth your love? Do I need to be doing all these things and feel happy about it? I don't; all I feel is tired and unappreciated. I'm there anytime someone asks me for help. Yet no one is taking care of me.

Why doesn't anybody see my worth? My kids and husband don't appreciate anything I do. They just keep creating more mess. People at church just keep asking for my help. Work just keeps giving me more things to do, when there are literally not enough hours in the day to get it all done. When will enough be enough? When can I rest? I'm so tired.

A Completely Exhausted Me

SEARCHING FOR WORTH IN DOING

When we are searching for our worth through our actions, we feel depleted after we give. We don't feel satisfied, and an expectation of something in return comes into play. We are expecting to find worth in our actions. Our value lies within. When we become aware of those internal messages playing in our heads, we recognize that we aren't doing things for authentic reasons. We are opening ourselves up to more pain and chaos. For some reason, the pain and chaos feels comfortable, or we wouldn't be pushing beyond what is good for ourselves. Our egos like to trick us into believing we are serving others when we are really fighting for our worth. We are trying to get from others what we are unwilling to give to ourselves.

Some people think having an ego means being full of yourself for your accomplishments, but egos can also show up when people are showing insecurities through their actions. When we can't get over our part in any situation, whether it is a success or failure, that's ego. Ego is our unconsciousness. That's why, when we question and become aware of how and why we are doing what we do, the ego's attachment to our happiness lessens. Our lack of self-worth, self-esteem, and self-image are all tied up in the grips of the ego.

I went from a child who loathed myself to an adult with a lot of unhealed baggage. I kept expecting the world to give me what I wasn't giving myself. I was trapped in the world of doing. I became drained. I couldn't understand why I was getting punished for doing so much and giving of myself. It didn't matter what I was doing; I never felt like it was enough. Why? I was punishing myself for not being good enough. I wasn't worthy of being a child of God. Our reasons may be different, but we only give ourselves away when something inside us tells us we aren't enough.

DIG DEEPER

Investigate your thoughts. Ask yourself:

- Have I ever considered myself a doormat?

- Have I ever heard myself saying something like, *I can't believe you did this to me after all I do for you*?

- Have I ever felt as though I give and I give and I give and get nothing in return?

LOOKING FOR OUR WORTH IN OTHERS...

Dear Partner,

Why don't you love me as much as I love you? I show you every day how much I love you. I give you massages. I make you breakfast, lunch, and dinner. I do your laundry. I buy you little gifts when I'm out and about just because I'm thinking of you. I write you love notes, get you cards, and put up reminders for you. What else can I do to make you want to give me the same kind of love in return? All you ever do is take, take, and take some more. I'm tired of trying to get you to love me. I don't even know why you stay with me.

A Frustrated Me

Dear Children,

Could you be any more selfish? You guys are a bunch of spoiled brats. All you do is take, take, take! You want everything to be handed to you, and the second I ask you to do anything you don't want to do, you act like ungrateful little assholes. Show a little bit of gratitude! I do so much for you. You have no idea what other kids have to go through just to survive, but not you. You get everything you want and you don't appreciate anything. I do your laundry; you throw it into piles in your room. I feed you; you tell me you don't like it. I clean, and you just keep throwing your crap down all over the house. You treat me like I'm a doormat you can walk all over. I'm so sick of being treated like this. I didn't do anything to deserve being so disrespected.

A Fed-Up Me

SEARCHING FOR WORTH IN OTHERS

- What are we expecting from others that we aren't giving to ourselves?
- Is it love, respect, value, or time?

If we are giving so much that we have nothing left, our boundaries and self-awareness are out of whack. There is some kind of war going on within. There is a direct correlation here to how we treat others. If we create war inside, we will create war outside. Others don't know how deeply tied we are to any one of our insecurities. Knowing our insecurities is not their job. A man or woman could say, "Wow, you must love food." Are you hearing that he/she is saying *you are fat*? Do you think, *how dare you*? He/she might have simply admired your taste in food.

We don't do for others what they can do for themselves when we have enough value in ourselves. We don't cover for them because we want them to love us. We don't rationalize and justify others' poor choices when we have value in who we are. We don't stick around to put up with unacceptable behavior if we see our own worth.

If our parents defined their worth by how much we appreciated them, we turn around and pass that down to our kids. This is part of the reason it may feel so natural. This happens generation after generation; we only break the cycle when we become aware.

Why do I treat myself like I'm unworthy of receiving love? This love can be from kids, romantic partners, moms, dads, communities, cultures, or even whatever Higher Power/ Spiritual Being you believe in. Once we ask the question, the answer will reveal itself in layers. Memories of past events might surface. People may come into our lives who show us that we don't take care of ourselves (not a fun one). We will feel unimportant to our children or people we take care of. We might think of all the times we volunteered to be in the service of others before we even considered taking care of ourselves.

We aren't capable of making others do what they don't want to do. We can't make anyone love us who doesn't. Forcing our value on others won't make them value us. When we stop expecting this out of others, we empower ourselves to make better choices.

BRINGING OUT OUR BELIEFS THAT SABOTAGE OUR AUTHENTIC JOY...

Dear Friend,

Why am I such a doormat? I keep letting people walk all over me, and they don't think twice about it. Maybe you're right; maybe I'm way too caring and trusting. I keep thinking I have this great person and then they will just keep letting me down over and over again. You're right; people don't change. He's never going to love me the way I love him. When we first got together, he made me feel complete. He was always complimenting me, and he put me high on this pedestal, making me feel like a queen. A few months later, and now I'm the one who is constantly working, trying to get him to show me his attention. Now, all he does is take. I not only don't feel complete, I feel depleted and deprived of love.

I guess I'm going to keep getting hurt because I just care too much. He said he thinks I need a night out with friends. I think him wanting to be with his friends is code for he doesn't want to be with me. Maybe he wants to go out with friends so he can find someone else. Why do I even care? Maybe I need to check his phone to see who he's been talking to.

I don't trust him. Even though he is just working and coming home, he must be interested in someone else if he doesn't want to spend all his free time with me. I told him he completed me, so why doesn't he want to include me when he goes out with friends? Why does he want time without me?

A Confused Me

SABOTAGING SELF-WORTH AND AUTHENTIC JOY

There are many beliefs we carry around to sabotage our self-worth and authentic joy. We can't stop getting in our own way until we see what is holding us back. Below are a few messages converted into beliefs that can keep us down. The more honest and detailed we can get, the faster we can break these destructive perspectives of truth, which is why this list is written in first person.

I'm a doormat. I let people walk all over me. I give and get nothing back. First problem: I *defined myself* as a doormat. I made doormat a part of my identity. I put my energy into being a doormat, so I started attracting situations where I could show the world I was right. I perpetuated the problem. I tell the world I have no value by lying down over and over again. I did it to myself. I didn't have boundaries, and I sought value in doing for others what they *could* do for themselves. I expected them to treat me as well as I treated them. The one I wasn't treating well was myself. When I love and value myself, I choose what I do for others wisely. When I change, my relationships change.

I'm too loving, too caring, too giving, and too trusting.
By believing this, I put out to the Universe that I'm going to suffer because I care too much. Then I get hurt and say, *See, it happened again. I was taken advantage of.* Having these "too much" beliefs makes me unconsciously search out ways for them to be true. Sometimes that means that, even when someone is being appreciative and grateful, I don't see it. I see everything someone else isn't doing because I'm focusing on spotting the negative. Being a loving, caring, giving, and trusting person is my gift to the world. The truth is I do "too" much when I'm not being loving, caring, giving, and trusting to myself.

I'm not complete. This one ties into my attachment to fairytales and being a hopeless romantic looking for *happily-ever-after.* The belief that there is another person out there to complete me takes away my power to be happy on my own. I've tied my worth to other people's feelings, thoughts, and beliefs about me. When they left, I would be devastated and go back to feeling like an incomplete waste of space. This is a vicious cycle of self-sabotage. *Great* teachers can be disguised as very dark human beings. I got to see exactly what happens when I look to someone else to complete me, and they never do. When I believe that it takes someone else to complete me, I don't see the men I'm with. I see an illusion of what I want in the happily-ever-after fairytale. It blinds me.

People can't change. I can't change. I can't do it. If I believe people can't change, I give myself the excuse that *I* can't change. I trap myself in the world of *can't*. When I say: *I can't be any different; I can't find a man who will love me the way I want to be loved; I can't be happy at work; I can't live the life I want to live*, those beliefs are sabotaging. Living in the world of "can't" has sabotaged me so many times. I can change my feelings, my thoughts, my perceptions, my actions, and myself anytime I choose.

DIG DEEPER

Make your list! Think back to your attachment to titles. Whatever your attachments are, apply them here. This includes negative self-talk that has turned into beliefs such as, I'm too fat, I'm too thin, I'm not smart, I'm ugly, I'm not good enough. All these beliefs are sabotaging the way you value yourself. If you don't value you, it will be hard to see and accept it when someone else does.

PROJECTING OUR FEARS TO THE WORLD...

Dear Women,

How dare you just sit around and let these men walk all over you! Can't you see what living in the white male privileged world is doing to us? You have to take a stand and show up to these protests and make sure men know we are not going to put up with their shit anymore. Women, you should be ashamed of yourself if you don't bitch-slap a man for hugging you when you don't want to be hugged. It's time for them to hear our rage!! Let's make them feel the way we have for so many years. We deserve the justice of seeing them squirm. Why aren't all women following me? We need to work together. We all have to stand together and fight! It's our time to show these men what all their suppression has done to us. We are DEMANDING change NOW!

They will see what happens when they don't change accordingly. Women, if you aren't standing with me, you're against me. You're just as bad as them. You're weak and conforming to this broken man's world. Your head is in the sand if you don't see my way of thinking. LET'S GO!!! HEAR MY ROAR!!

An Enraged Me

PROJECTING OUR INSIDES TO THE WORLD

What we project out, we get back. The worse we feel about ourselves, the more drama and chaos we attract to our lives. Is that really what you want? The good news is that you're the one person you are capable of changing. No one else needs to change in order for you to better your life. Just you. We can't shift until we become conscious of what we are already projecting and see how those projections are feeding our beliefs about ourselves. How we live inside is what we create outside. The more we see ourselves as the creators of our own stories, the more we realize that we are in charge of the trajectories.

If we are projecting negative images to the world, we are deflecting our low self-worth onto others. We are projecting our lack of value by trying to make ourselves feel more important. Since we don't see our own value, we are trying to force others to see us. We don't even recognize how negative we are being to our romantic partners, friends, family, coworkers, and with strangers on social media. We are living unconsciously. When we are genuinely kind to ourselves, our perspective on humanity changes. When we feel genuinely good about ourselves, we don't try to take someone else down. What we might not realize when we are stuck in the feeling of lack is that our attacks are really aimed at the person in the mirror.

When we try to force change and don't know the energy we are projecting, we get stuck repeating the lessons over and over until we learn from them. If we have any kind of anger, rage, fear, and hate toward ourselves, we project that. We find ways to attract that image back to us. It could be in our intimate relationships, family, friends, coworkers, communities, politics, and causes we are representing. We wonder why we aren't being heard, but are we listening? Are we hearing what we are projecting?

We can't be empowered until we fix the relationship with the woman in the mirror. People won't listen to what we have to say until we listen to ourselves. Once we really investigate our relationships with our beliefs, and ourselves, we get to start taking our blinders off. We can be open to the possibilities of changing the things that don't work for us, but best of all, we stop trying to force change on others. We see it is our example, our energy, and our love that will attract them to our messages. Think about being a child. What had more of an impact: how the people around you lived or how they told you to live?

OTHER PEOPLE'S LIVES...

Dear Stranger,

I can't believe you reported harassment five years after it happened. You are just looking for attention. It's the perfect time to get your five minutes of fame. You should have reported the situation right when it happened. I would have reported it. If it really bothered you, you should have pressed charges then. Coming out now, you should be ashamed of yourself. Why didn't you just tell him at the time?

A Know-Better Me

Dear Friend,

You should leave him. You can't keep putting up with his shit. You are better than that. Why are you still there?

You are being stupid for not leaving. If you really want to leave, just leave. I would have left a long time ago. I would never put up with all that shit. Listen! If you're not going to go, I can't talk to you anymore. I'm sick of hearing the same thing over and over when I already have told you a million times what to do. I'm literally at the point where I'm not sleeping at night because I'm stuck in your life. I don't want to be in all your drama. I told my husband the situation and he says that your life is ruining our marriage. He doesn't want me talking to you at all. He says he is sick of me getting so worked up about what is going on with you. I just really can't understand why you haven't left him. You could have left a thousand times already and you are still choosing not to. It is either not as bad as you say it is, or you're just a complete idiot. I would never have let it go this far.

A Know-Better Me

FOCUSING ON OTHER PEOPLE'S LIVES

When we think we know how someone else *should* be living, what they *should* be doing, how they should be acting, when they *should* be doing something—and the why is because we know better—we are deflecting and avoiding the one person we can change. When we are *should-ing* someone else, we are doing the same to ourselves. We use should, would, and could as tools to shame/guilt ourselves and others. When we go to bed thinking about them and fixing their problems, we are the problem. We have attached to their story. We've taken on their journey as though it's our own, and it's not.

Doing this is different from giving advice when it's asked. When we are doing what is described above, we are attaching to the outcome of someone else's story. We know what is best for them. We think WE can fix them (ego). When we can't fix them, we take it personally, like it is our failure. When we are simply giving advice (when asked), supporting them, assisting them in finding the tools they need, and speaking from our own experience, we acknowledge that it's their journey and it's up to them to redirect it if it's not going in the direction they want it to go.

When we try to FORCE change on others, we are not accepting their journey as theirs. We are actually stripping them of their value and worth during a vulnerable time. That doesn't make us better people; we are showing others how sick we are. We don't shame and guilt others if we are healthy inside. When we attack, it shows who we are. When we are shoulding others, it is a great time to look at how we are shoulding ourselves.

Our projections don't help support them or us. If we are focusing on other people's lives, we are not conscious of the story we are writing for our own life. We are over there trying to run their life, while ours is internally and many times externally falling apart because we are not giving our lives the attention and focus.

When we're conscious of our own journeys, we empower others to make the choices that are right for them. Our worth isn't tied to what they decide to do on their journeys. We don't become victims because someone isn't following our advice. Do you sometimes wonder why a person is coming to you and yet not listening to your advice? The person is listening. You gave the person a seed. They may plant it; they may put the seed in their pocket for later. They are venting because they are processing their situation. It doesn't mean they are ready to change anything yet. Celebrate the progress that they are making. Talking about what is hurting us is a step in awareness.

DIG DEEPER

Should. Would. Could exercise. Pay close attention to anytime you use the words should, would, or could. Whether you are talking to yourself or others, answer the questions, but REMEMBER, this is not an exercise to use to beat yourself up.

- How is using these terms serving your self-worth?

- Are these words being used to shame or guilt others?

- Are using these words making you feel better than or less than someone else?

- Are using these words truly helpful to the situation you're in?

- Are using these words helpful to serving humanity?

- Are using these words helpful to bettering yourself?

- Does using these words help you feel better about yourself or others?

WHEN OUR INNER VICTIM TAKES THE WHEEL AND FEAR WINS...

Dear World,

I'm scared of you. I keep getting hurt and I'm in constant pain. I'm scared of everything. I'm scared to live and I'm scared to die. I don't know why I keep getting put in these situations where I see the worst in people. It started with my family. They abandoned me when I needed them the most. They let a predator take advantage of me. If I can't feel safe in my own home, with my own mom and dad, then I will never feel safe. Every time I start feeling close to anyone, I question what he/she is going to do to hurt me. Friends let me down at every turn, bosses take advantage of me, and don't even get me started on my romantic relationships.

Men are my enemy. They are all just a bunch of predators. They all want something. I just need to stay as far away from them as I can. I refuse to let a man in ever again. They are destroying our communities, our country, and our world. They have to be taken down. I'm tired of being their doormat to be walked all over. I'm not going to be your victim anymore!

A Fearful Me

EMPOWERING THE VOICE OF OUR INNER VICTIM

The inner victim wreaks havoc in our lives, many times without our even knowing it, because we justify our right to be a victim. This is a very common belief for minorities, including women, LBGTQ people, and people of different races and religions. Part of the reason this mentality runs strongly through minorities is because many of us, our families, and our friends have been victims of prejudice, harassment, or abuse in one form or another. Healing from our traumatic pasts is not a simple or easy journey.

The only person who keeps us a victim is in the mirror. It starts with us. Sometimes when we are the victim of a violent crime, whether mental or physical, we find some kind of safety in staying in a victim role. We cover ourselves with it like a blanket, and the way we keep the victim alive is by becoming a victim of our own selves. Then, in turn, we project this victim onto the world. We struggle to trust, feel secure, and safe. We attack, even when we aren't being attacked, out of the fear of being attacked. For instance, *I'm going to hurt them before they hurt me.*

We don't trust ourselves, so we can't feel safe to seize opportunities or take risks. Then we take it out on our partners for not being trustworthy, when we projected the distrust by attracting them in the first place. We relive the trauma over and over. Now, this can also be a medical dilemma like PTSD. Thankfully, there are a lot of different resources to help us rewire to stop reliving the traumatic experiences. The first step is becoming aware of the fact that we are letting a past event(s), trauma, or person live in our present life even if it is over.

How is your inner victim serving you to be better? Victim mentality blinds us from experiencing authentic joy and experiencing love because, when we project our inner victim, we project a world of fear. It is all we see. We will see where we are victim over and over. This is a brutal path, filled with ample amounts of pain and suffering, but only we can choose when we are done with it. When we shut our minds to the possibility of changing and seeing different perspectives, we are fighting to keep our victims alive. We will continue on our fight against, giving it power to create more chaos for ourselves and others. Solutions for positive change come from peace, love, joy, and acceptance. We play into our inner victim's hands when our judgments take control and we start fighting for what we are against and lose sight of our vision to be better and to do better.

PART II

ACCEPTANCE OF WHAT IS

'The most attractive thing about the Buddha was that he saved one person: himself. That's all he needed to save; when he saved himself, he saved the whole world.'[2]

—*Byron Katie*

2   Byron Katie, Hope Beneath Our Feet: Restoring Our Place in the Natural World, ed. Martin Keogh (Berkeley: North Atlantic Books, 2010), 190

Chapter 4

HEALING AND RELEASING THE PAST

BEING AFFECTED BY EVERYDAY ENCOUNTERS...

Dear Driver Who Cut Me Off,

I forgive you for being so tied up in your own world that you weren't paying attention to my passengers, my car, or me. I have been there too. You are probably in a rush, and I know your actions were about where you are and not where I am. You didn't do this to personally attack me. For that, I forgive you. I pray that you and the other drivers around you get to your destinations safely.

With Acceptance,
A Better Me

Dear Customer,

I forgive you for being so distracted that you didn't look at me. You have a mission, and I could tell your mind was in a million places. I know your inability to acknowledge the person in front of you has nothing to do with the person I am. If you had looked at me, you would have seen my smile of understanding. I pray you are able to slow down enough to stop missing the great moments in front of you.

With Acceptance,
A Better Me

EVERYDAY ENCOUNTERS

When it comes to forgiveness and releasing the past, *START EASY!* Don't go for the big ones yet. Forgiveness takes practice. As for the guy who cut you off, you may at first say a few things to yourself while banging the steering wheel. Then, all of a sudden, remember to work on forgiveness. You may lie down in bed... *Oh, forgiveness!* Don't beat yourself up.

Sometimes we take daily encounters so personally that we carry them around all day, telling anyone who will listen, *"You won't believe what just happened to me!"* We've been trained to be resentful for a long time. It is deeply imbedded. Some of us were marinated in the womb with resentment. Be patient with the process. Laughter is a great way to release some of the toxic build-up that happens when the unknown driver, cashier, or customer catches us up in our story of being victimized. When we are fully ready to release the pain of the past, we will.

If you think back to all the anger, fear, and rage stirred up in Chapter 1, you may have felt it somewhere in your body (stomach tightening, chest clenching, or fists tensing). The longer we hold onto these feelings, the more layers we add. What we are doing by releasing the past is shedding layers and layers of toxic weight.

Visualize putting on ten heavy winter coats. Feel the weight and heat. The restriction is so bad that you can barely move. Every movement becomes a struggle. Now, some of these coats are beautiful on the outside. They are your protective armor to the rest of the world. Their beauty can lure people in, then *bang*; the coat inflates to create a giant wall around you. The "*you*" it is protecting doesn't get hurt—*at least that's what you convince yourself is true.* We are love, and the coats are the fears and resentments that we are holding onto. When we shed the layers, we show the world the love that is who we are. Removing the layers takes time. Don't be hard on yourself when you don't get it right away; keep making the effort.

If we want the changes in this world that are best for humanity, we must release the toxic energy we are holding onto from the past (even if it was five minutes ago). We can't carry around that kind of fire without people getting burned, including ourselves. Our messages of change can get lost in the anger, rage, and fear that are driving us. For some, it will trigger traumatic reactions that perhaps stem from parents yelling at them during childhood. If we are coming at others with the energy of our unhealed past, they will react with the energy from their unhealed past. Instead of bringing out the humanity in them, we bring out children with wounded egos. Then it becomes a battle of control. *I'm right and you're wrong.* Through forgiveness, we find compassion.

WORKING THROUGH MEDIA TRIGGERS...

Dear Media,

I see how your show is trying to trigger my fear. I believe your security is invested in it. You won't get it today. I will look at all the stories you show me with compassion and an open mind. I will not take your word as gold. I forgive you for trying to make us conform to a fearful way of thinking. I know I have showed you my interest in looking through eyes of fear countless times. That is my responsibility to monitor and be aware of. If I can't find a way to watch you with eyes of compassion for all parties involved, I will stop watching you because holding onto all this fear is not in my best interest.

With Compassion and Acceptance,

A Better Me

Dear Sexual Harassment / Assault Perpetrators.

When I watch the news, I see how much they want me to hate you. I can tell they are looking for my rage to come out. I admit, when I saw the news I was triggered by my own past, and the thought of hating you became very appealing. I wanted to hate you for what happened to me. I didn't know how prevalent this behavior still was in today's world. I didn't understand how many women this has affected.

I find a sense of comfort knowing I wasn't alone. I feel my voice growing inside me wanting to create change, so this cycle of harassment and abuse can end. I will not feed on your anger. I will be filled with the love and bravery of all the people who are supporting each other through this time of change. I'm encouraged to show my love to those who are seeking to break the cycle. I won't let you be a reason to hate men. You will be the reason I want to help educate the ones who didn't know the pain they were causing. You will be the reason that I give love to those who are suffering. Seeing you being held accountable shows me that I don't have to be the victim of my past anymore.

With Compassion and Acceptance,

A Better Me

MEDIA TRIGGERS

In Chapter 2, you got to see how we trained the media to be what it is today. Now, we need to find ways to hold onto our compassion while watching the news. When you see something that disturbs your inner peace, question your judgments on the people involved:

- How do you find compassion in the worst of circumstances?
- Is the media trying to enrage you?
- Are they trying to trigger your fear?
- Is this where you want to be?
- How can you turn a horrible situation into something positive?

Forgive people for their ignorance, for not knowing better. Forgive the news media for feeding on the fears of humanity. Forgive the person who is struggling so hard in their own world that something they did had a negative effect on another person or a community. *Instead of hating them, pray for them.* Pay attention to the way changing your perceptions affects your body and mind. We don't have to carry around other people's unhealthy choices. We don't have to make villains out of the media. We choose the energy we put into what we are watching. Choose wisely!

ISSUES WITH OUR FAMILY HISTORY...

To the Father Who Abandoned Me,

I've thought a lot about you over the years. I felt rejected by the first man who was supposed to love me. I have to say, that left a mark. I didn't understand how I could have meant that little to you. I didn't understand how you could be so heartless. I've made a lot of mistakes with men in search of the love I never got from you. I put my worth in their hands and every time they didn't love me back, I felt the pain of you leaving me all over again. It took a long time to even see that I was looking for you through my relationships with them.

I've had to learn a lot of hard lessons in love. I used to believe that love hurt, but now I know better. You weren't healthy enough to be in my life. You actually did me a favor by not being there, because I would have had years of rejections instead of just one. Not because you didn't love me; you didn't love yourself. You weren't capable of giving me the love I would have wanted from a dad. My worth has nothing to do with your actions. My worth is my gift to myself. I deserve the love I give to myself. I will take responsibility for the love I put into the world, starting with me.

Thank you for being who you are so that I could discover the strong and beautiful person I am. I can now feel free to love a man without an attachment to you.

With Acceptance and Love,

A Better Me

To the Addicted Parent.

I used to hate you. I would look at you in utter disgust as you lay there, too tired to spend any time with me. I was embarrassed because I never wanted my friends to see you stumble, fall, and be out of it while we all tried to act as normal as we could. I hated walking on eggshells, not knowing what your mood would be. I was angry for having to take care of you and your needs while mine went unmet time and time again. You weren't the parent I wanted to have growing up. I was resentful because I felt I deserved more than what I got from you. I couldn't understand why I was continually left to fend for myself. At the time, I had no idea what good could come out of the harshness of my childhood. I thought you and God hated me.

I felt alone and out of place while families gathered to support their kids. I waited for you to show up. I was disappointed again and again. I felt abandoned. I searched for the love I wanted from you in my personal relationships, a cycle of disappointment and hurt. I turned the rejection into self-hatred. That's when it hit me: I can choose to follow your path of self-hatred by clinging to the story that I'm unlovable, or I can rise above it. I choose to rise above it.

I will embrace the love within myself. I will see myself as a child of God who is loved for being the person I am without having to be or do anything. I will see myself through the eyes of the purest love there is. I don't have to repeat any of your patterns of loathing. I will embrace a new path with love at the very core. I accept my past and the lessons you taught me about how I want to live. I'm sorry you chose the path you did. I hope one day you will decide there is a better way, but that is your journey.

On my journey, I will look beyond the expectations of the parental role. I will see you as having a sickness. This will keep me from taking your poor choices personally. Your choices have nothing to do with me. Thank you for helping me see the dangers of taking the path of addiction and self-loathing. I know because of your example that I don't want that for my life.

With Acceptance and Love,

A Better Me

FAMILY HISTORY

Good old Mom and Dad! If we wanted to, we could get lost in some intense blame cycles here. Many of us have. See how it feels to say, "*Thank you for the lesson,*" instead of, "*I'm like this because of you.*" When we feel those deep-seated resentments crawling up, we have a choice. We can see the feelings as an opportunity to grow or a curse to fail. When we're blaming, we are investing time in negative energy. Our egos LOVE that. We make some of our worst decisions when we're stuck in this energy cycle. We look for love in all the wrong places. We seek our worth in other people. We get caught up in one addiction after another. All the while, nothing is our fault and we are victims of our childhood[3]. If we want to be healthy adults, we need a shift in perspective from victim to heroine. Some of the most challenging people are our greatest teachers.

---

[3]   This isn't directed toward people who suffered severe childhood trauma. Not because it doesn't work the same way, but because childhood abuse can create increased trauma and might take a lot more than letter writing and self-reflection. Though it has worked for some. Trauma therapy is an AMAZING tool for trauma recovery. Don't be scared to ask for help.

GOING DEEPER

Reverse the blame. Look back to your childhood from a healing perspective.

- What did my childhood teach me?
- How can I do better?
- What positive traits came from my upbringing?

HEALING WITH LOVED ONES...

Dear Addicted Child (Adult),

I'm sorry that you found your way to addiction. That is a tough path, and, once you're on it, choices feel limited. I had to realize that I can't rescue you from this. You are on this path for a reason. The best I can do is to show you by example that there is a healthier and happier way. I can't preach it to you. I just have to live my life the best I can and show you what is possible. I will let you know that I love you, but I can't enable you. You must be the one who takes back control of your life. I know you are capable. If I keep rescuing you from yourself, I'm telling you that you can't get better without me. The truth is, you can't get better if I'm in control. I will just perpetuate the cycle that you aren't good enough, and you *are* good enough. You have to experience your own consequences in order to grow from them. I know you are capable of living a better life, but you have to choose to. I can't do it for you.

I will be here to love you and to listen, but I know when you are ready to stop, you will be driven to get the help you need. I must see you as the adult you are instead of the child I was responsible for. You are old enough to make your own decisions. Your successes and failures are leading you on your journey. I don't know what is best for you because I don't know what you are meant to learn from this path. I love you and hope you will discover you are worth more than you are giving yourself right now.

Until you figure that out, you will continue to suffer. No one else can complete you. You are a whole person all by yourself.

With Acceptance and Love,
A Better Me

Dear Addicted Friend.

My heart breaks watching you being consumed by this disease of addiction. I know your addiction has nothing to do with me. I forgive you for being self-centered, self-destructive, and self-sabotaging. I know the *you* I love is buried under the disease. I can't change you. Only you can decide when you are ready to end your addiction's power over you. I hope you get the help you need. Please forgive me if I put distance between us right now. I have to take care of my own well-being, and your negative behaviors aren't a safe place for me to be. I love you, and I hope that one day you decide to come back to us.

With Acceptance and Love,
A Better Me

LOVED ONES

Our children can be mirrors of where we are inside. How we treat them reflects what is going on inside us. Sometimes we are overcompensating and enabling them (doing what they can do for themselves). Other times we aren't doing enough, which shows a lack of motivation because of something going on in us. If we aren't getting enough sleep, we might not feel the energy to take care of our parental responsibilities like meals, hygiene, and quality time. We neglect them because we are neglecting something in ourselves. If we are dealing with adult children, our self-worth and self-image go down if we put our worth into how they behave.

- Do we feel less good about ourselves if they are addicts or mentally ill?

- Do we feel shame if they were hurt and we were unable to protect them?

- Do we blame ourselves for their life choices?

These are all signs that we have a lot more healing and letting go to do. I'm still a work in progress. When it comes to stressful interactions with my children, I still have to watch for when I'm measuring my value by their actions. When I do, I see that I have more work to do on healing my own self-worth.

Our friends and partners are also a reflection of where we are. Consider these questions:

- Are we doing too much to get them to like/love us?

- Are we saying yes when we'd rather say no? Oh, and then resenting them for it?

- Are we trying to fix them instead of supporting them on their journey?

- Do we treat them as though we know what's best for their lives?

- Are we attracting people with a lot of drama?

- How are they treating us?

Just by checking in with ourselves, we're ahead of the game. We see when and if we are putting expectations on others to do what we aren't doing for ourselves. We see how we are treating ourselves by how we treat and are treated by our loved ones. We are living our purpose by healing ourselves. A healthier us equals a healthier world.

UNDERSTANDING PERSONAL TRAUMAS...

To the Boys Who Hurt Me in Childhood.

I was taught that when a boy is mean to you, he likes you. Your views of me affected me so much that I put all my self-worth in your hands. I listened when you told me I was ugly or gross. I changed myself repeatedly—I was trying to be someone who was liked by you.

This belief damaged the way I entered relationships with boys, and eventually men. The belief also damaged the way I saw myself with respect to my relationships with men. I gave boys and men power over me for a very long time. I felt the effects of this both in the workplace and in my personal relationships. I would lose myself every time I entered a new relationship, trying to be the girl who would be loved by you.

I went into work feeling like male coworkers needed to find me attractive to see my work. I put on a show, and I would change according to how they treated me. I accepted unacceptable behavior in the office just to feel wanted or noticed. All this started in my childhood as I tried to get your attention. I see now how my beliefs about you projected out to the world I created for myself. I realize now that you were just being a kid who didn't know any better. Your actions were reflections of your world. I'm the one who chose to let them create mine. Looking back as an adult, I can see clearly now.

Since I blamed you for everything that went wrong in my relationships for so long, I learned to blame ALL men. I treated every man as if he was damaged. I started accepting men treating me badly, expecting that every man would. I didn't know that only unhealthy men treat women badly. I had no idea that love wasn't painful. Injured people try to hurt other people. If I was healthy, I wouldn't have put up with the negativity and hurtful words and actions. I would know without any doubt that I deserved better.

I will never be the change I want to see if I don't let go of your influence on me. You are just another human trying to figure out how to live this life in the best way possible. I forgive you for your mistakes. I know they weren't a personal attack against me. Thank you for being a part of my journey to help me see that my self-worth must come from within, or I will be the victim of someone else's own lack of worth.

With Acceptance and Love,

A Better Me

Dear Abusive Partner,

Thank you for showing me how poorly I thought of myself. You showed me that my worth must come from the inside. I'm working on that now. I know I don't deserve the horrible things you have said and the manipulations you've used to keep me down. That is your illness. That is you trying to gain some sort of worth by making me feel less than you. The compassionate side of me empathizes with the pain you must feel in order to hurt women the way you do.

Though I see the good in what I've learned about how to take better care of me, I'm not where you are anymore. I know my worth. I need to take care of myself now. I need to show myself the love I deserve. I won't accept your abuse anymore.

With Acceptance and Empowerment,

A Better Me

Dear Sexually Harassing Boss,

My hope is that the unacceptable way you treated me was in ignorance. I want to believe that there is a compassionate and naïve person inside you who has no idea how wrong his behavior is. That is why I will tell you that I don't accept your advances or harassment. They don't make me feel safe, comfortable, or respected as an employee. I don't want to believe that the way you judge me has anything to do with how you see me sexually. If you appreciate my work ethic, communication skills, and dedication to my position in the company, I ask you to respect my personal boundaries and treat me as a respected employee. If you feel you can't do that, I will have to go above your head to handle this matter because I am too valuable and talented to put up with inappropriate behavior. I'm really hoping that you didn't do this intentionally to try to belittle me.

I'm hoping we will be able to start a new page and that this will help you, not only with me, but with all female employees, present, and future. I can promise that you will get a higher quality of work by being respectful and appreciative of the assets we are to the office. Thank you for your time and careful consideration of how you will move forward.

With Respect,

A Better Me

PERSONAL TRAUMAS

Some traumas can feel too hard to forgive. Just the thought of forgiving the wrongs of people who have committed rape, abuse, assault, murder, kidnapping, and terrorism may be too great to bear. Releasing the toxic energy about the actions they committed is for *you*. Instead of focusing on forgiving, we can come to a place of acceptance of what happened. Then we can search for different ways of looking at it so we aren't carrying around the trauma.

Being a survivor of rape, sexual harassment, and abuse, I get it. I need to get personal with you. I transformed my views on how I saw my trauma in the world. I saw their presence in my life as an important lesson for me to grow from. I learned to see past their actions and focus on healing myself and supporting others.

I can still get fired up when it comes to assaults on women, among other triggers. I'm not perfect! It's not my job to be perfect. I take responsibility for the toxic energy I spread, accept my part without blaming, and then keep doing the best I can WITHOUT BEATING MYSELF UP! I support women in finding their self-worth during and after abuse. My experiences gave me the gift of compassion. I understand why women don't leave abusive situations. I see how they are treating themselves. I hear their pain and feelings of worthlessness. I've felt trapped and without any choices. I don't contribute to being a part of a woman's shame cycle (saying they're stupid or insulting them) for not leaving. I know it's their journey.

My compassion helped me to see that when someone is spreading toxic energy, they are wounded. Experiencing traumas taught me to see a person behind their wounds. I did a lot of things that hurt people when I was submerged in my own pain state. Choosing to change my perspectives on my past changed my whole world. It helped me see the empowered woman within.

GOING DEEPER

Letter Burning. Letter burning is a practice I use when I'm feeling angst. I write a letter getting everything out. I go outside and say a prayer. One I use is, *"I'm calling on you to help me to release my anger and frustration so I can forgive. I don't want to hold onto this energy any longer. Please take it away. Thank you, Amen."* I watch the letter burn. I imagine the toxic energy shifting into love as the Divine takes the energy away from me.

If you do this, be safe and follow safe fire rules.

RELATIONSHIP WITH THE DIVINE...

Dear Divine Source,

Thank you for all the opportunities that you give me to grow. I can grow closer to you by embracing the compassion of the people who share experiences of authentic love, or I can fall farther from you by embracing the path of fear. I choose the path of love. I would like to say that I always notice people's love, compassion, empathy, and understanding, but I don't. I do my best. However, I do notice the outpouring of love when I read stories about communities coming together to support one of their sick members. I notice that, when a natural disaster strikes, so many people stop thinking about what's happening in their personal worlds and reach out to help those who are suffering.

I'm moved by men and women who spread messages of love through books, TV, seminars, and movies, sharing the stories that make us want to be better humans. I know all these gifts of love come from you.

Humans make mistakes, and there are some who have bad intentions. I trust you will place the right ones in my path to learn lessons in courage, strength, and perseverance. You may have to take some of my loved ones with you, but I know they are safe. Their purpose now is to be with you. My purpose is to remember the good times and loving memories to take with me as I support others who suffer the same sort of loss.

I'm sorry for all the years I feared you. I'm so grateful to be in your loving grace. Thank you for sending me messages through people, books, and entertainment that remind me you are ALL love. Every situation you bring to me has love at the core; I just have to find it. I felt whole once I saw that the more I loved myself, the more I could love you and the people you created.

Thank you for showing me that there is no RIGHT way to experience your presence. I have direct access to your love. I honor you by loving myself, supporting others on their journeys, and letting go of the negative energies that don't serve you. If I'm spreading a message of fear, I'm not serving the LOVE that you are.

With Love, Acceptance, and Gratitude,

A Better Me

SPIRITUALITY

Accepting the past, letting go, and embracing *what is* through a perspective of love is a spiritual practice. We are one with spirit anytime we express authentic love. We must let go of what doesn't serve us to make space for more love and compassion. Why would we want to stay in a place that keeps us from being one with the greatest source of love? If we don't feel worthy of the purest source of love, we aren't at one with the Divine Source. If we aren't one with the Source, we can mistake authentic love for misguided fear. When we open our minds to healing our wounds with love, we leave room for the Divine to come in. The more peaceful we are inside, the more open we are to connect with the Divine's messages of love and compassion. Connecting to the Divine Source through fear is an illusion.

When I watch bombings, terrorist attacks, sexual assaults, and death, along with natural disasters and more, I see the world unite. I see compassion and love come alive from individuals all around the world. I revel in people seeing past color, country, man, and woman. I embrace the true meaning of humanity. I don't like that it took events like these to get us here. But I CHOOSE to focus my energy on the good that came after—the love and prayers the world spread. Doing this has also helped me heal one of the most important relationships in my life, and that is with the *Divine Source of love*. This is how I take care of the energy I'm projecting.

GOING DEEPER

Come back to this chapter. Letting go of the past is also a great place to come back to when you are ready to take off some more layers. You will get exactly what you are supposed to get each time you read it. Accepting where you are is part of developing your own personal spiritual journey. Don't put any undue pressure on yourself to be farther than where you are. The deeper the trauma, the more layers you will have to peel. Doing too much too fast could make you unstable and make you want to retract into your safe places. If this is where you are, that's okay. You have the seed and know where to go when you're ready. The beauty on the other side is beyond anything you could ever imagine. It's time to start letting go!

FOR THE WOMEN HEALING SELF...

Dear Me,

Wow, you have made a lot of mistakes up until now. But take heart, each one has led you to being a better version of yourself. I watched you work hard at dealing with lingering feelings as they came up in your everyday life. You pay attention to your reactions to others. You've taken traumatic situations as opportunities to heal and grow. I see you doing your best to let go of all your past anger, rage, and resentments. I'm done expecting you to be perfect. I'm sorry that I haven't had compassion for you. You deserve the same compassion you've given to so many others. I know you learned from your mistakes and paid high prices for some of them. You are a better person now because of your experiences.

I forgive you for putting your worth in other people's visions of you. I realize now that you are the only one who must believe in yourself and your abilities in order to have a better life. When I see you through eyes of love, I'm not seeing all the things you did wrong. I'm seeing you in this moment, the way you righted your wrongs, the kindness of your heart, and the loving nature you kept buried in fear of someone taking it away. I've uncovered your worth.

I understand that no one can ever take away that part of you. It doesn't matter who loves you or who thinks you're worthy. That is their business. You are nurturing and loving you the best you can. I want you to project the love you have inside.

It's time to let go of the perceptions of the past that created an injured version of you. We don't need her anymore. Embrace the woman you are right now. You are love. You are being the best version of the **you** that you want to be.

With Acceptance and Love,

A Better Me

SELF

When it comes to forgiveness, sometimes the biggest challenge is to forgive ourselves. When we don't forgive ourselves, our shame and guilt projects into everything we do in the world. Our relationships suffer; our causes suffer; the world suffers; we suffer. If we are rescuers, martyrs, and doormats, we are codependent on others to give us what we aren't giving ourselves—LOVE! We can only be depleted by our service to others if we aren't serving ourselves first. When we give to ourselves first, we see clearly how to best serve others. Sometimes that means letting them do for themselves.

Forgiving ourselves is a huge part of this equation. We get so full of our own shame and guilt that we give beyond our limits of what is healthy. In order to heal, we have to release ourselves from our pasts and forgive ourselves for the mistakes we made before we knew better. Some of these mistakes will go back as far as we can remember. We didn't know better. *WE DIDN'T KNOW BETTER.* If we knew better, we would have chosen better. It's time to let go. No matter what we have done, we all deserve the love we want to give everyone else.

This section of the book takes time. Don't rush yourself or feel like you have to complete this before moving on with the rest of the book. Remember the example of the coats. The practice and process of forgiveness happens in layers. We may take off one layer but be too scared to take off the next one because we don't know if we will be secure enough without it. We have built up years of defense mechanisms and protective walls using these coats of armor. We must feel we are safe before we can take off the next layer.

When I got healthy enough to leave my abusive situation, I was in a better place than I had ever been. My practices of forgiveness and letting go were getting stronger and stronger. I felt proud of the woman I had become. Life showed me I still had a lot to learn. I didn't learn until a few years later that my need to pick men who wanted to be rescued was *my* codependency. I was still seeking value outside of myself. I was volunteering and feeling depleted if I couldn't make things better for someone else. Finally, I saw that I was holding onto layers of guilt and shame that were making me feel like I wasn't a good person. This became evident through my futile attempts to rescue and save men to prove my worth (I laugh now thinking about how much trouble I got myself into). If *I* can release myself from my past, you can too. It's not an easy road, but it's definitely worth it.

Chapter 5

BUILDING SELF-WORTH

ACCEPTING WHO AND WHERE WE ARE...

Dear Me,

I accept me where I am today. I see the effort I've put into being the best version of myself. I can see the progress that I'm making on a daily basis. I don't expect to have the perfect life or do everything perfectly anymore. If I were supposed to be somewhere besides where I am right now, I would be there. I have something to learn through all the challenges I'm facing. I accept that, with any negativity that comes toward me, it is my choice whether to add it to my story or not. I don't have to give other people the power to affect my self-worth.

The only person who has to accept how and when I feel happy, peaceful, and joyful is me. I don't have to let any situation define my worth. My worth is in my perception of me. I'm the only one who chooses the messages I tell myself. I can make them positive or negative. The decision is mine! I accept the responsibility of taking care of me. I commit to being conscious of how my thoughts are sabotaging me, how my attachments are hurting me, and how my fear is tearing me down. By accepting all of this, I give myself the power to change.

With Love and Acceptance,

A Better Me

ACCEPTANCE

Stay open. Stay open. Stay open. Before we can create positive, long-lasting change, first we must become aware, then accept. Our self-worth is tied up with a very persuasive ego. Let the layers come off naturally. Forcing change is a part of our self-sabotage. We think we have to change all of our unhealthy patterns at once, then we can't keep the momentum, we start slacking in one area or another, and then all the changes we were trying to make fall by the wayside.

If you are trying a bunch of new techniques, it's okay to let some fall off. It's okay to make one change at a time. Accept where you are on your journey, wherever you are. These are some of the patterns you will notice as you become more self-aware:

- You catch yourself after you beat yourself up
- You'll catch yourself in the act
- You'll start catching the thought when it comes up and redirect yourself
- A new pattern that's beneficial to your worth emerges
- Your healthy pattern becomes a natural response

There isn't even an urge to belittle or call yourself a name. This could take weeks, months, years, or decades. This is your journey. You will be where you are supposed to be at any given moment. Allowing ourselves to be where we are is what it means to be in *acceptance*. If you are expecting yourself to be somewhere you aren't, you are still in the broken cycle.

People show up in our lives for a reason. When we stop trying to resist their purpose in our lives and accept that they are there for a reason, we grow and expand. We also *accept* when it is time for them to go. It's important to see that there is no wasted time. We learn to be better by seeing ourselves at our worst. Trust the learning experience.

If you struggle to break unhealthy patterns, don't be afraid to ask for help. Pray for support, release the outcome, and be open and *accepting* of how the prayer is answered. You will be amazed at what solutions start presenting themselves to you. Trust that you will be led exactly where you need to be to get the help you need in breaking these harmful patterns. You may have already asked for help. This book might have showed up in your life in some unexpected way to answer a question you put out to the Universe. This happens all the time.

GOING DEEPER

Pay attention to signs from the Universe. When we want to change and live in acceptance, we get signs to lead us to changing for the better. The signs may be a trip to a library, a meditation practice, a community, an inspirational video, an unhealthy person (lesson), a book, a meme, a website…the possibilities are endless. Say a prayer to help lead you and stay open. The key is *accepting* that the answers to your prayers for change are available to you. Don't get caught up in outcome. Focus on the journey.

CHANGING OUR SELF-TALK TO REFLECT THE HEROINE INSIDE US...

Dear Me,

I'm taking responsibility for the way I talk to you. I'm the one who keeps the messages alive. I had to believe the negative messages in order to create a reality around them. I'm the one who needs to change the messages playing in my head. No one else can do it for me. I have to show myself I'm worth the energy that I give to everybody else. It's time for me to be my own heroine. I'm writing my story now!

Here is what I love about the heroine I've created: She is smart. She knows when she has choices. She can learn and grow at any moment she chooses to. She is confident. She knows how to make decisions and stick to them. She treats herself with love and respect. She gives to others only when she knows in her heart that it is the right thing to do. She is brave. She cries openly when she is moved and is not ashamed of her tears. She makes a difference in other people's lives by simply being herself. She is loving and kind to the people around her. She listens. When people have a different opinion than she does, she doesn't try to think of what she's going to say next. She listens and asks questions about what she doesn't understand. She's beautiful, not because of what she looks like on the outside, but because of the heart she shows the world. She shows immense levels of integrity, good will, compassion, and faith. I love who my heroine represents. I love being her.

With Love and Empowerment,

A Better Me

SELF-TALK

By now, you've become conscious of your self-talk and how it affects your life. Just as it took time to develop the process of tearing ourselves down, it will take time to start bringing ourselves up again. We have to make positive self-talk a habit. The reason is that negative self-talk is deeply embedded. Making an effort to do more positive self-talk doesn't mean the negative won't sneak up on you. What you will find is that it becomes less and less. Make positive self-talk a practice until there is no negative self-talk in your vocabulary. Here's the challenge:

1. EVERY day for the period of time you choose, between twenty-one and ninety days (commit to the number of days before you start), write three things you like or love about yourself. You can write more, especially as time goes on, but commit to at least three different things every day.

2. Find one inspiring quote each day to go with your list. You can find them on social media, in a book (like this one), or online through a search. Just take the time to find an inspiring quote. It doesn't have to be about anything in particular, it just has to inspire you.

That's it! Just two steps that you can add to any practice you are already doing. I will tell you, it's really fun to do with friends, because you start spreading the love too—*bonus!* The inspiring memes being passed back and forth becomes a habit too, which tends to give them more power to inspire. However you choose to approach this challenge, focusing on what you like and love about yourself is one of the most important steps on this journey.

GOING DEEPER

Self-worth collage. Make a self-worth collage out of words from magazines that inspire you. Think of how words, sayings, and quotes represent the way you want to see yourself. Cut them out and paste them on the base of your choice. When you're done, put it where you can see it.

To My Ideal Partner,

Thank you for being the amazing partner that you are. You know how to give me love anytime I need it. You make me laugh even when we are disagreeing. You are an artist and enjoy using your creative mind to come up with solutions to problems. You allow me to have the spiritual journey that is best for me without judging me for it. You look out for my best interests, yet you don't force me to do things I don't want to do. You are generous with your love and your time. You make me a priority in your life. I know without a doubt how much you love me because you show me through your actions. Your touch is so gentle, tender, and authentic. Your words only offer backup to what your actions say. You are brilliant. You know how to think outside the box to solve all kinds of challenges. You are beautiful and inspiring inside and out. You take care of yourself and live a healthy lifestyle to maintain the energy you need to go out on amazing adventures.

I love that you enjoy going on adventures with and without me. We give each other the space we both need to have quality time together, alone, or individually with our friends. I love the way we enjoy listening to each other's escapades and how much we trust each other to do right by our love and our friendship. We are respectful in our communications, whether we agree or disagree. We allow each other the freedom to be ourselves, and we love each other for the people we are. Your love makes me smile and keeps me uplifted.

I commit to showing you love, compassion, trust, and loyalty. I love you!

With Love and Gratitude,

A Better Me

IDEAL RELATIONSHIPS

Some of you might look at this title and think that it is in the wrong section. What do the ideal relationships have to do with self-worth? Basically, it's much easier to look outside of ourselves for inside answers. Many of us still have some old programming in us saying, *It's selfish to think of ourselves first.* If we have even an inkling of that thought, we put ourselves very low on our priority lists. We attempt attracting partners or friends who can give us what we're lacking (the feeling of completeness), but we find that our partners are toxic and our friends are judgmental. When we lack self-worth, we can put up with a lot of bullshit from other people, because we put up with a lot of bullshit from ourselves.

When we think of our ideal partners and friends, we are actually seeing what we want in our ideal views of ourselves. Looking at what we want to get out of other people shows us what we're not giving to ourselves, and it also can show what we appreciate about ourselves too.

If you are someone who gives herself away as much as I did, you might discover that, until you look at this list, you aren't doing or making time for any of the activities you like to do. You might find you have done nothing to invest time in your own joy and peace. I saw that I was putting off things I loved doing because I was waiting on the perfect partner to do them with, yet I wasn't attracting relationships with people who liked to do the things I liked to do.

When we see the person we are looking to find, we have a blueprint for what we need to do for ourselves to change the energy we are putting out there. We need to work on letting ourselves shine the way we are ALL intended to.

GOING DEEPER

Define your ideal partner. Think of what the absolute ideal friend or partner would be for you. Answer these questions (substitute gender when applicable):

- How does the person present himself?
- How does he treat me?
- How does he treat me when I disagree with him?
- What does a disagreement look like with him?
- How does he treat himself?
- What kind of foods does he like to cook and eat?
- What are his best emotional qualities?
- What would he do to show me he loves me?
- What does his spiritual practice look like?
- How does he take care of himself?
- Does he let me get away with mistreating myself?
- How does he inspire me?
- What are his thoughts about managing money?
- How does he talk about me when I'm not around?
- What does he like to do for fun?
- What do we like to do together?
- What is his education level?

- What would the ideal vacation look like with him?

- What is sex like with my ideal partner?

- What kind of art do we appreciate or participate in together?

Really dive in, write pages if you need to, but MAKE SURE you are writing about what you actually want in an ideal friend or partner. Just to give you an idea, my list was around four pages. Lay it all out there! We won't attract those people until we become those people. Now take the list and start doing the work. How can *you* become everything on that list? You will see that you already have some of these qualities. Others you might need to do some work. Some may have you saying, *Oh, shit!*

THE MOST IMPORTANT LOVE LETTER...

Dear Self,

You are incredible. I love being in a relationship with you.
Thank you for making the time to take me on walks,
meditate with me, and create amazing meals with me.
You are so much fun to be around. I love the way you can
see the beauty in life. Going on a nature walk with you
is so relaxing and peaceful. I really get to enjoy every
moment and remain completely present. You are so great
at showing me how much you love me by taking the time
to take care of me, body, mind, and soul. I love when we
sit down and read a book that inspires us to be better. You
come up with so many creative ways to start doing more
fun things.

I feel great inside when we are spending quality time
together. When I'm present with you, my mind feels clear.
Decisions and solutions come to me so much more easily.
When I'm true to you, I feel peaceful. You are there to lift
me up when I feel the chaos starting to swirl inside. You
show up with your love, compassion, and patience as I
work through life's lessons. We continue to come out
stronger on the other side. You are my rock star! Thank
you for being on this life journey with me. I love you.

With Love and Gratitude,
A Better Me

LOVE AFFAIR WITH SELF

When you look in the mirror:

- Who is looking back at you?
- Would that person be the partner of your dreams?
- Would that person do anything to make sure you feel happy, healthy, and loved?

If the answers are no, the great news is you are looking at the one person you can change! It's time for the most important love affair you will ever have.

I hope you completed your ideal partner list. The more you become the woman you want, the better your life becomes. This is an investment of time and energy like any new relationship would be. Just like letting a new partner in your life, you and only you can decide if the person you're courting is worth your time. We are the example of how we want other people to treat us. If *you're* not willing to give yourself the time, why should anyone else? We make the time for the people and things that matter to us. We don't come up with excuses. We find ways to fit in the person or activity. You have to be important to you in order to create the time for this important love affair.

Stop waiting for someone else to do the things you want to do. If you like going for hikes, go hiking. If you like riding your bike, go for a bike ride. If you like to take long drives along the mountains or the coast, go do it! Go to the beach or lake and watch the sunrise or sunset. If you like road trips, take them. Cook the foods you want to cook. Don't say, "Cooking a lovely meal is too much for just one person." You deserve a gourmet meal (even if you have to clean up all the dishes, too)! Eat at the places you want to eat at. When we learn to love our own company, going to places alone empowers us to feel free. We get to choose our experience. We can thank the Universe for creating whatever beauty we see. We can write ourselves the love letters we always wanted to receive. Leave yourself loving notes around the house for some daily inspiration. Create a romantic space to sit and read a book that will make you feel good about where you are. You deserve the greatest love story. Give it to yourself!

GOING DEEPER

Take yourself on a date. Take yourself out to do something you enjoy. What have you been waiting on a partner to do for you? Do it yourself. Enjoy a day, night, or even a weekend out. Enjoy your own company. Give yourself the time and effort you deserve!

THE JOURNEY OF SELF-CARE...

To the Best Version of Me,

I see the importance of taking care of you—body, mind, and spirit. I commit to taking the time to show you my love by nourishing all the best parts of you and healing the places that aren't working in your best interest for the life you want. I commit to focusing on you instead of shifting blame and judgment onto others or using that blame and judgment against myself. I will look at you with compassion and patience as you find your way and continue on your journey. I will be there when you are struggling with your darkness to remind you that you are valuable, worthy, and lovable. You are deserving of my love just for being you. You are complete! You are whole! Your struggles have made you stronger and, as I reinforce positive and loving messages of courage, strength, experience, and hope, you become more secure in the beautiful person you are.

If you happen to forget some of your self-care routine, I will not criticize you for it. I will meet you with compassion. By doing that, I'm giving you the self-care you need in the moment. My compassion for you expands the more I let go of the past patterns of thought I've held onto for so long. The more time I spend loving you, the better I will be able to take care of you.

Thank you for being patient with me on this journey. My worth is growing daily. The more confident I am in myself, the greater my life becomes. I see more blessings and opportunities to love and honor the woman I am. Thank you for being on this journey with me. You are the best companion and friend I could ask for.

With Love and Gratitude,

A MUCH Healthier Me

SELF-CARE

Once you have invested the time in yourself to have a love affair, self-care becomes a lot easier. It takes on a natural quality, and we stop shaming ourselves into taking care of ourselves. When we love ourselves, and we don't like the way we feel, we find a way to feel better. If we are full, we stop eating because it doesn't feel good to eat anymore. We see how sugar is affecting our day with the highs and lows, so we become more conscious of what we are putting in our bodies. We don't want the goal of exercise to just be self-acceptance or to change the person we are; we do it because it simply feels better and our bodies work better when they are healthier.

The basics are that we want to take care of our bodies, minds, and souls/spirits. Self-care is going to look different for each individual. It is not our place to judge what other people do; our job is to keep our own grass green. We are all different; we can't expect self-care to look the same.

With self-care, our personal boundaries become clear and easy to read because our energy matches what we are saying. We don't put up with unacceptable behavior. If we need to say something to the person who did it, we do. If we need to go above their head, we do. If we need to walk away, we walk silently and without guilt or shame. We don't take in what other people do as a personal attack on us, and we don't respond with shame and guilt.

When we are taking care of ourselves, we *KNOW* we don't deserve to be treated disrespectfully. We make choices to handle the situation in a way that makes us feel good inside. We stop fighting against peace by attacking others for their unhealthy life choices. Self-care is about keeping our peace inside, so we can create more outside.

GOING DEEPER

Self-care toolbox. For every day, or when you are struggling, you can pick just a few simple things to work on taking care of yourself.

- Create a self-care journal.
- Define what self-care means to you.
- Make a list of all the ways you can take care of yourself: body, mind, and spirit. Keep the list handy.
- Do at least three things for yourself a day to honor your self-care. These things don't have to take a long time. They just have to be for you and only you.

Self-care is a journey. You aren't going to do it perfectly. If you are overwhelmed by the prospect of making time for yourself, pray about it. Now, you just did one thing for self-care. You are reading this book, so check two. If we are making self-care complicated, there is a resistance going on. Investigate that resistance and that is the third check mark for the day. Each step in awareness and acceptance is progress.

FEELING THE LIGHT OF THE UNIVERSE...

Dear Universe,

An amazing feeling of authentic joy is rushing through me. The love within me is overflowing to the point where waterfalls are coming out of my eyes. The beauty is majestic. I tingle from head to toe. The hair on my arms and legs is standing on end. My body feels weightless. In my connection to you, I am pure energy. No thought in my head is left untouched. If I imagine what infinite love and gratitude would feel like, it is what I feel when I'm connected to your energy. *I am complete!*

I'm getting everything I need. Everything is and was as it should be. I am one with my journey. I'm not fighting any piece of me. I feel complete peace.

Universe, I honor and appreciate being connected to you, and I will remain open to it happening again. Abundance is rushing back into me as I'm here with you.

With Love, Light, and Abundance,
A MUCH Better Me

SEEING THE LIGHT

Our light inside has the ability to shine brighter than any of the darkness around us. Our light comes from the love inside us. The stronger the love, the stronger the light. The love we have for ourselves is the amount of light we can give to the world. If we want to support the healing of our friends, family, community, and world, we have to heal ourselves in order to brighten our own light first. Fear acts as a dimmer switch on our light. The more fear we have inside, the more darkness takes over our lives.

When we are in the light of our lives, there is an authentic joy that emanates from our very being. We can break out into a giggle or a joyful cry in an instant. We don't get this because of trying to find some outside way of making ourselves happy. It comes from deep inside us. The light illuminates our spirits.

In meditation, we might actually see the light and feel like we are being lifted to a different place, a heaven on earth. Love is our salvation. Fear is our hell. If we are fighting to see the light, we won't see it. If we are fighting, there is fear. If we are in fear, we do not trust our Creator, the Universe, the Spirit inside of us, however you choose to look at it. Seeing the light is the most authentic place of love we can be in. No force is on the path to seeing the light.

The first time I remember experiencing the light in full effect was during my love affair with myself. I was so overwhelmed with joy while meditating. The light was effortlessly running through me. It was a completely different feeling from when I've done guided meditations, visualizing a light and having it work through me. That took mental effort to keep the image in my head. There was no force when I saw this light. I wasn't trying to visualize anything. I just felt it and then saw the vision of it so clearly, as if I were looking at the light shining through a window on a bright day. I realized that, at that moment, I felt complete and whole for the first time on my own. I wasn't trying to be anyone more than who I was, and I fully loved her.

HOW GIVING FROM A LOVING PLACE CHANGES THE WAY WE FEEL INSIDE...

Dear Self,

I'm committing to start giving from a loving place. I no longer want to play the role of victim, martyr, and/or doormat. I understand now that I did that to myself. I didn't honor myself, and I neglected my own boundaries by walking on myself. Self-care comes first! I will honor myself and make choices that are best for me. I will give when it feels good to give, and, if I sense ulterior motives or have expectations of other people based on what I do, I will stop and question whether it's right for me to help or not. I will change my perspective in order to give to myself and others with love.

If I begin to feel resentful toward a person I'm giving to, I will question my thinking. I will look at how I'm not showing myself love and respect by my actions. I'm not the victim of other people's reactions. I need to make sure to honor and feel secure and confident about my own choices.

It feels great when I'm giving to others from a loving place. I feel good about myself. I don't feel taken advantage of or unappreciated. I'm also seeing that the people I'm giving to are more appreciative of what I am choosing to give. Yet knowing that doesn't make me feel complete anymore. I am already complete. It's just an added bonus that seems to increase the positive flow of energy around me and through me. Giving from a loving place builds my confidence, creates healthy boundaries, and helps me share the authentic joy of supporting the people and community I love.

With Love and Gratitude,

A Better Me

GIVING TO OTHERS FROM A LOVING PLACE

Be true to who you are! Self-worth is the key to giving from a loving place. If you have love in your heart and are honoring your own mental, spiritual, and physical needs, you will make the best decision in that moment and learn whatever the moment is meant to teach you. You can't do that if you don't love, respect, and trust the person you are. Trust the process.

Giving to others from a loving place fills us with energy. We don't become martyrs, credit-seekers, or depleted from giving too much. We aren't doing it to fulfill any obligations from church, groups, family, friends, work, or community. We do it because a love inside us calls us to give. When we don't feel the authentic call, we check in with our boundaries, the event, the person, and/or the reasoning. We decide if it is the right thing to do for our own well-being. This doesn't mean we will avoid anything that risks our personal safety. Checking in means we will listen to the call. If we do things for the wrong reasons, our minds, bodies, and spirits suffer. When we do things from a loving place, we are in complete trust of anything the Universe brings our way. We may feel pain that has a great lesson to teach us. We may struggle more than we ever knew we could, which will bring out our confidence and strength. We may reach points where we say, *Why did I agree to do this again?*, or *I'm scared*, but deep down we know we are exactly where we are meant to be.

Giving from a loving place empowers us. It doesn't mean that, if we go that route, it will take us on the path of happily-ever-after. But it will lead us to living an authentic life, to feeling authentic joy, and being present during authentic pain when the pain is necessary to feel in order to change and grow. Pain is an essential part of the journey. As we get healthier, we may feel less and less pain, but, if we are trying to avoid the pain, we are running away. That is where we can give power to addictions or the quick fixes. If we are running, we can't give from a loving place because fear is running us. We will give with the expectation of feeling a certain way, getting something in return, or becoming worthy in the eyes of our Creator.

Chapter 6

BRING IN THE GRATITUDE

RELEASING THROUGH GRATITUDE...

Dear Past,

I'm so grateful for the person I am today. I wouldn't be this person without you. I've learned so much through all my pain and suffering. There were times when I thought the world would be better off without me. Yet I kept living. I kept pushing through. All the negative energy I put out there came back to me, and I'm so grateful I could see it. I was given lessons time and time again to show myself love and compassion. It may have taken getting hit over the head with an emotional two-by-four in unhealthy relationships. In time, I was able to find myself. I could leave unhealthy or toxic situations with my head held high, and for that, I am SO incredibly grateful. I'm grateful I learned that my value doesn't come from what anyone else thinks of me. I learned everything I needed to in order to be the person I am today.

I'm no longer a prisoner of what was. Accepting and releasing my past has inspired me to be the best version of myself. In doing that, I'm finding my way to use what I've learned to contribute to the betterment of humanity. My experiences taught me to have compassion for others who are faced with their own personal darkness and challenges. I'm able to show them love without enabling them because I remember what my journey looked like and how I could only take the steps I was ready to take. That also enables me to observe and not judge. Now I have only compassion for those who are still in toxic relationships. I know why she doesn't "just leave him" or "just quit."

I have patience for the learning process of personal growth. I don't expect people to be perfect. I also have hope, because even when I was in my pits of despair, I came out on the other side. I'm beyond grateful through all my experiences, I can smile and laugh bigger than I ever thought was possible. Where I once used my tears to cleanse my soul, now I cry tears of joy to fill it.

With Love and Gratitude,

A Better Me

Dear Ex-Lover (who is a narcissist or abusive in any way),

I used to think I wasted my time with you. Now, I'm grateful for the experience. I got to learn about myself. If it weren't for you, I wouldn't have seen what I needed to work on to become better. I'm grateful to see how putting each other on pedestals blinded us to the people we were. I'm grateful I could see how important actions are instead of depending on empty promises. I'm grateful I learned about everything that love wasn't, so I don't have to repeat the same patterns. It's because of you that I'm able to spot what is healthy and what isn't. I'm so grateful I can see red flags clearly now. I know what to watch out for in future partners. I know that if I'm attracting and pulled toward unhealthy individuals, I have something to work on.

My time with you was like enrolling in a class to make me stronger. I am now! I'm grateful that I finally feel like the strong, courageous, brave, smart, and beautiful woman I knew was buried under all the rubble of self-doubt and self-abuse. I'm so grateful for all the lessons that got me here. Your words no longer have power over me. Your opinion no longer defines who I am. I'm so incredibly grateful for the love I have inside me now.

With Lots of Gratitude,

A MUCH Better Me

RELEASING OUR PASTS

Our pasts are over. When we learn from our experiences, we can find gratitude even in the darkest corners. How we view our pasts is a choice of perspectives. We are choosing how to write our own stories by where we put our focus. When we focus on gratitude, our stories may take dark turns, but we will be led back to the light.

The ego doesn't like authentic gratitude. We remove ourselves from the drama of a situation any time we can find gratitude to release us from the weight of being a victim of our pasts. How are you telling your story?

- When you were in school, a boy was cruel to you. For years, you fought self-esteem issues, feeling like men saw you as a gross, disgusting loser. You have choices: you can continue to be a victim of this boy who is long gone from your life, or you can be grateful to have learned that your worth doesn't lie in someone else's hands.

- A boss harassed you when you were in your early twenties. You can continue to be hostage to this experience and, in turn, allow all your male bosses to turn into unconscious enemies as you live with the fear of what happened in the past. By doing this, you let the victim cord dictate your present moment. This means your fear is creating an energy that is hurting you both psychologically and physically. The person who hurt you isn't suffering, why should you have to? You can choose to be grateful that your new boss keeps professional boundaries. You can be grateful that you have grown into a woman who feels comfortable and clearly states her boundaries.

We also don't need to continue to be victims of ourselves for any poor choices we've made in the past. Yes, we have all made mistakes. Did you learn from them? Be grateful, you learned a lesson. Are you repeating the past? Be grateful you are getting another opportunity to make better choices. Are you stuck in addiction? Be grateful for the programs out there that can support you in stopping when you're ready. You can be grateful for friends who will listen over and over as you try to find your way to become a healthier and happier version of yourself.

Just as we can choose to be the victims of people, places, or circumstances (unrelated to crimes against us), we can be the heroines who write our own stories and are willing to release anybody and any situation to the grace of gratitude. This is a choice, not always simple and not always easy. No one can make this choice for us. We get to choose how to interpret our pasts and all the people involved in them. Being in gratitude releases us from anyone who has put us in a situation where we were once his or her victim. We don't have to keep carrying the weight that comes from those traumatic events.

GOING DEEPER

Create a gratitude journal. Every day, make a list of things you are grateful for. Don't just say it, WRITE IT DOWN! Start with a minimum of three, and then watch the list begin to expand. If you do this one thing EVERY day, you're moving away from living in lack and projecting, manifesting, and attracting abundance.

CELEBRATING OUR DIFFERENCES THROUGH GRATITUDE...

Dear Self,

I remember when I used to criticize you for being different. Now, I'm incredibly grateful you are different. We need people to be different. I'm grateful for the lessons in accepting myself, and having patience, tolerance, and compassion for others. I'm grateful for the day I stopped taking my differences personally. I don't have to feel attacked for being different or having different beliefs from someone else. Others don't have to be any more or less than who they are and neither do I. I love the freedom that comes with accepting differences. I'm grateful when I get the opportunity to learn about someone else's lifestyle and culture. I get to see love in so many different forms by simply appreciating differences among us all.

I'm grateful I wasn't made the same exact way as anyone else. It challenges me to find our similarities. I find every person has loves, fears, joys, and pains. If I make an effort to see them, I see me. It reminds me that I'm not alone. Whatever I choose to focus on grows. People's differences teach me what I want and don't want for my life. I get to choose. How can I not be grateful for that choice? I can choose to be a victim of my differences and create separation, or I can choose to celebrate my differences and expand my love. I'm grateful for my right to choose the way I want to live.

With Love and Gratitude,

A Better Me

EMBRACING WHAT MAKES US DIFFERENT

As easy as it can be to criticize ourselves, being grateful is SO MUCH less painful! Just like with our misery, the more we dish out, the more we get back. Why not choose to be grateful for what makes us different, instead of attacking ourselves and others for it? When we reach a point where we can be grateful for our own differences, we find a place of compassion and acceptance of other people's differences.

We aren't all going to like and believe in all the same things. Life would be so boring if that were the case. We wouldn't have as many opportunities to grow and evolve if we all lived life, looked, and thought the same way. When we live in gratitude, we can celebrate our differences and see our internal judgments of ourselves and others as learning opportunities. We can be grateful for getting to learn about how brains function where there is trauma, abuse, mental illness, deformity, addictions, oppression, and/or entitlement.

We can be grateful for opposing opinions and beliefs regarding politics, religion, gender, parenting, cultures, different countries, and/or lifestyles. When we are in gratitude, we are open to learning. We are open to seeing better solutions to problems that are hurting humans, animals, plant life, sea life, and our planet as a whole. We are living a life as a better me, which contributes toward a better life for anyone whose life we touch. We create a better world to live in. Our part is to let the positive seeds of change grow inside of us and hand them out to those around us. We don't have to force anyone to plant them; we can simply be grateful for the opportunity to pass along our kernels. It's the recipient's work to figure out what they want to do with them. If they have the right atmosphere in their gardens to let them grow and flourish, the seeds will be planted. Their garden is going to look different from ours, but that doesn't mean it is any less beautiful. We also all have weeds to sort through. Don't judge someone else's weeds: take care of your own!

ACCEPTING WHAT IS WITH GRATITUDE...

Dear Oppressors,

I'm grateful you are where you are. The response to you has shown me the darkness that has been pushed down. I'm grateful for the opportunity to face not only my darkness, but the darkness of the people I love, as our opinions of you differ. Some of us have been sitting back and watching from the sidelines. Now the energy I'm seeing in the world has given myself and others the courage, strength, and hope to work toward making a difference. By asking many questions of the people who support your oppressive tactics and those who don't, I could see how much fear was out there. I'm so grateful that you have helped to unite people who were feeling alone and scared. You gave hope to people seeking change. You've raised awareness of how internally and externally divided many of us still are.

We are seeing changes happening all over the world. Some that were expected, and others many of us did not see coming. Either way, I'm grateful for what your tactics are igniting in me. I am ready to create positive changes in my life, and I needed to be faced with seeing what feels right for me. Seeing the damage that acting against other people can do was essential to my growth in becoming a better version of me.

With Appreciation and Gratitude,

A Better Me

EMBRACING WHAT IS

We may not be able to change what is happening around us right now, but we can see the opportunities we are given to make changes for a better tomorrow. That doesn't start with fighting what today has already brought us. If today makes you feel uncomfortable, sit with it and ponder:

- What can I learn from what is happening right now?

- How does what I'm doing right now contribute toward what *I don't* want?

- How does what I'm doing right now contribute toward what *I do* want?

- How does what is happening right now make me want to change what I'm doing?

By asking ourselves questions and adjusting the questions to fit the situation, we can be grateful for the awareness that the current situation is bringing us. Without where we are right now, we can't get anywhere else, for better or worse. That is why each moment we are in matters. Our thoughts in each moment create momentum. Which way you take the momentum is up to you. I didn't say this would be easy. Accepting life as it is right now can be a huge struggle, and then adding gratitude to it—I know!

Where are you right now? The reality is that you have exactly what you need in this very moment. Be authentically grateful for what you have in your life right now. Once you become truly grateful for what you have, your whole mindset starts transforming. Our moments make more sense and our obstacles start lessening. With all the extra energy you get from not living in lack, you can put your attention on things that help people, animals, and the environment. Now you are attracting more positive energy to those outlets, and you have even more to be grateful for. Once again, where we are right now has value. Seeing life through eyes of appreciation and gratitude brings purpose to what is and opens us up to endless possibilities for positive change.

LETTING OUR INNER LIGHT SHINE...

Dear Journal,

I'm grateful for each breath I get to take today. I'm grateful for a roof over my head, the feeling of being safe, secure, and protected. I'm so grateful to have eyes to see clearly, ears that hear laughter, and legs that can hold my weight. I'm grateful for the cool breeze and the swaying trees. I'm grateful for being alive. I'm grateful for the opportunity to support other women on their journey to discovering their worth. I'm grateful for my patience with men who don't get the importance of it. I'm so grateful to the men who are on this ride with us and becoming better versions of themselves. I'm filled with joy and gratitude to pass down a legacy of love.

I'm grateful for the time I get with family and friends. I'm so happy and grateful to be able to give and receive love from a loving place. I'm grateful for the kindness of

166 | Letters from a Better Me

strangers and those who trust me enough to share their pain. I'm grateful for opportunities to serve humanity. I'm so happy and grateful for each woman who finds her worth and gets to see the miracles that come with the transformation.

I'm grateful for every time I get to see a hero in action. I'm grateful for the pay-it-forward drive-through lines at fast food restaurants. I'm grateful for the men and women who are called to be first responders. I'm grateful for the people who are serving others through their long-term care. I'm grateful for Republicans, Independents, and Democrats, because each party can bring us awareness and challenges to find solutions. I'm grateful for all the different religious groups who serve through love. I'm grateful for narcissists who taught me to be strong and love myself. I'm grateful for situations where I can learn about myself and others. I'm grateful to be an empowering voice of inner light.

With Love and SO Much Gratitude,

A Better Me

EMPOWERING THE VOICE OF OUR INNER LIGHT

The more we focus on gratitude, the more powerful our inner light gets. Let's take Oprah as an example. She didn't start where she is now. In the beginning of her career as a talk show host, she struggled to find her path. As her inner light got brighter and she worked to break down her walls of fear, her inner light didn't just shine—her voice began to reflect her inner light's brightness. The focus of her talk show shifted as her light got stronger and stronger. She started attracting all these *amazing* teachers to her. If we are attracted to her, our lives get brighter too. Her shift helped us to get out of our own ways. Her light got so bright that the network she was with couldn't shine bright enough. She manifested her own network—OWN—which projects the light coming from her.

On my journey, I've been brought back to Oprah countless times, who has guided me to books, meditations, individuals, and organizations that have played a part in my journey. Her light helped to brighten my light. That is the power of living in gratitude. Our lights don't just get brighter, our voices begin to be heard. Our light is our power.

Every time we choose to live in gratitude over fear, we feed our light. Every time we come to a situation with love, we strengthen our voices. The more we live in gratitude, the more power love has to shine light on fear, which is the darkness inside of us. Appreciating our fear and darkness for what it has to teach is just another way we make our lights shine brighter.

CREATING ABUNDANCE THROUGH GRATITUDE...

Dear Universe,

I'm so overwhelmingly grateful for all the abundance you've shown me. As I began writing my gratitude lists, I could see just how much I have to be grateful for. I don't feel like I'm without anything that I need in this moment, and when I need more it shows up. I'm in awe of your ways of making sure I'm provided for in each moment. I'm grateful for opportunities to see abundance of love, spirit, friendships, familial bonds, compassionate strangers, financial means, places to explore, adventures to take, and an overall amazing life to live. I couldn't have this without living in gratitude. When I lived in the constant wanting, I was incapable of seeing all the abundance you have for me. I used to come to you from a place of lack; now I'm overflowing with love and appreciation for all the gifts of the present moment.

With Love and Gratitude,

A Better Me

LIVING IN ABUNDANCE

Abundance is the outcome of living in gratitude. The more grateful we are, the more abundant we are. Our relationship with our circumstances dictates whether we live in abundance or lack. Abundance keeps us giving and receiving from a place of fullness. We're not worried about impressing people to fill a void; we are full, complete, and abundant exactly as we are in this moment. We are SO grateful for all the blessings that have brought us to where we are right now. When we are abundant, giving from a loving place is easy and natural. We are also able to receive from others without feeling shame or guilt. We know that the people who give to us are being filled too. Their giving extends the cycle of gratitude and abundance.

Living in fear doesn't lead to abundance. That's why the richest person may not ever feel abundant. Living in fear requires us to live in lack, which is the opposite of abundance. Abundance tells us we have everything we need in this moment. Lack tells us there is always something more needed to make us happy. When we live in lack, we look to the outside to fill us. We keep making and spending money, while continuing to feel like something is missing from our lives. We feed on the cycle of fear that keeps us lacking.

Let's take the life of a single mom. Imagine this single mom has a horrible relationship with money. There is never enough money, so she can't have a social life; she works three jobs to make ends meet, and she is constantly depleted and tired. She forces herself to do it all on her own and she doesn't like help from anyone because getting help means she's weak. She's angry with God, because she feels like she works so hard only to continue suffering. She doesn't feel like she's getting anywhere in life. I think we've met this woman before; heck, she might seem a little too familiar.

Okay, same mom, different attitude. She is grateful that she has the opportunity to work and contribute to her community. She's grateful she can show her children how to make it, no matter what life throws at them. She's grateful to meet so many people through the work she does. She makes time for friends because it is important to her and it feeds her soul. She's grateful she can be with her kids and that she can provide them with food and a safe place to grow up. She's grateful to God for the opportunity to learn, grow, and become a better version of herself so that she can show her children a positive example. Living in gratitude creates abundance. The love flows into her life so she can nurture herself, her loved ones, and her community. She's full of love, so she gives love and gets love back. When we are full of love, abundance follows. Staying on that path leads to miracles.

SEEING THE PATH TO POSITIVE CHANGE
THROUGH GRATITUDE...

Dear Creator,

In my gratitude, I find clarity. I see the changes I can make to do my part in caring for our planet and the life on it. In my clarity, I found my inner peace. In my peace, I can create positive change. I'm not attacking or pushing myself on others who are not ready for what I have to say. I can be the example I want to see and be aware when my energy is moving into war internally or externally. I'm so grateful for the awareness that helps me find my way back to peace. The more I focus on gratitude, the more I embrace who I am and what I stand for. My communication with people is open. I listen and find solutions because I'm not just seeing my own way. I'm grateful because there is a lot less stress in the solution mindset.

I can see when I'm supposed to act and when I'm supposed to remain silent. The blessing comes from knowing I'm exactly where I'm supposed to be. Living in love and gratitude has given fear the back seat in my life. I'm driven by solutions that inspire more love. I'm grateful for every step I take toward positive change.

With Love and Gratitude,

A Better Me

BECOMING OPEN TO POSITIVE CHANGE

When we live in gratitude, our path to positive change becomes clear, even if we can only see the next step to take. We see it without confusion, shame, guilt, or obligation. We aren't thinking about what we should be doing, what should be happening, or how we should be treated. We simply appreciate what the lessons of the past and the present have to teach us, and we honor the call inside us through gratitude. Our journeys to positive change means finding purpose in the steps we've taken, what we've learned, and taking the next step.

Think about all the different jobs out there. There are some jobs you know you wouldn't do, wouldn't want to do, or don't have the education to do. It takes all kinds of people with all kinds of different paths to fill the job market, right? We need all of them. The same goes for any cause, charity or volunteer work we are drawn to. Just because one person is called to take a stand about one thing doesn't mean it is what everyone should do. If we are shaming others into doing work for positive change, we are living in lack and fear. We are not trusting that the people who are supposed to be there will show up. That shame and force are actually putting negative energy into a positive cause. The more negativity goes into it, the less people will hear the message of positive change.

We stop this cycle by bringing gratitude into our own personal journey and any cause we are supporting. Think about the difference it would make if every meeting started out with gratitude. The trajectory of the meeting has a better chance of flowing in a positive direction instead of getting stuck in all the problems. When we are in a place of gratitude, we appreciate the input that is brought to the table. It can help us stop thinking about what we are going to say next and focus on what we can learn from the person talking instead.

Who knows? The solution may be in the room just waiting to be heard.

Creativity thrives on being open, appreciative, and grateful. If a person feels safe to communicate their ideas, it creates more creativity within the group. The group strengthens. Now, a group can strengthen a bond in love or in fear. It takes listening, observing, and being aware of what we are contributing to know which power we are feeding. If we want to create positive change, we have to stop contributing to the fear.

PART III

TAKING CHARGE AS AN EMPOWERED WOMAN

'I was once asked why I don't participate in anti-war demonstrations. I said that I will never do that, but as soon as you have a pro-peace rally, I'll be there."

—Mother Teresa

Chapter 7

WHO ARE YOU AND WHAT DO YOU STAND FOR?

EMBRACING OUR WORTH...

Dear Me,

I used to feel like a doormat. I believed the people who said that compassionate and loving people got hurt more. I created a reality around that belief and I kept attracting people who would prove it right. I didn't understand that, once I stopped treating you like a doormat, nobody else would be able to. The horrible way I was being treated had nothing to do with the kind, compassionate, and loving person I am. It had to do with how I treated you. I neglected you to serve others. I chose to follow beliefs that fed fear, and I created a reality around that fear.

Loving you helps me find my power to create a reality I want to be living. I'm living from an authentic place where I am in full understanding of how my thoughts, feelings, beliefs, and actions are creating my path. I have the power to change anything that isn't working, but I lose that power when I lose my connection with you. If I'm not connected authentically to you, all my relationships suffer, including my relationship with the *Divine Source* of all love. My relationship with you determines whether I see through eyes of love or fear. If I choose fear, I become confused and get lost and distracted among the countless examples of manifested fear in the world (hate, greed, envy, misplaced power, and corruption).

I love you! Thank you for showing me the magic that a relationship with you creates in my life. I'm ready to face the world and discover solutions to the challenges that come before me. I'm ready to be the loving, compassionate, and creatively powerful *being* I am created to be.

With Love and Gratitude,

An Empowered Me

HOW DO YOU WANT YOUR LIFE TO LOOK?

We get what we put our energy into. If we are putting our energy into what we lack or what we're against, that's what we'll get. If we put our energy into our abundance and what we are for, we will get more of that. Our lives reflect our insides, for better or worse.

If we want positive change, our hearts and minds need to be focused in the positive energy we are cultivating. We need to tap into the energy of what the reality we want looks like. Letter writing is a tool that can be used to help build ourselves up, find the healthy relationships we want to have, and put the right energy into the causes we are supporting.

Now is our time to embrace the magnificent women that we are and what we have to offer the world. It's not anyone else's job to see our worth. We have to know what our magnificence looks like. Be open to seeing yourself as the best possible version of you.

- What does she look like?
- How does she represent herself in her family, community, relationships, and career?
- What does she uniquely offer the world?
- How does she treat herself with love, honor, and respect?

GOING DEEPER

Define Love. In Chapter 2, we discussed some of the confusion around love and what it is. Now it's time to get fully clear on that definition and take an honest look at how we are supporting love in our lives. Once you find your definition, sit with it and brainstorm ways to represent yourself and what you want to contribute to the world. Corinthians 13:4–7 was the clearest definition to me. Find the definition that resonates with you.

FEEL WHAT IT'S LIKE TO BE THE WOMAN OF YOUR DREAMS...

Dear Me,

Wow, you have come a long way since you started this journey of self-discovery. Look at your life now. I love the way you stand tall and navigate how and when to assist the people who are brought into your life. You used to get walked on, and now you have the sense to know whether what you are doing is truly serving the best good, for you as well as the person you're serving. You can discern when it's better for the person to find their way out of their situation and when your support is building them up to make better choices to become stronger.

You're amazing at offering a positive perspective when you hear people gossiping or judging others. Your mind is focused on seeing the best in people and allowing them to be human and make mistakes without that determining their worth. I know you used to get caught up in that kind of stuff sometimes—no judgment. I love the person you are now. You know how to be there for people in a healthy way, and you're a wonderful example of what healthy boundaries look like.

You don't say yes when you feel ambivalent about doing something. You really are true to yourself and your needs. You make sure you take care of *you* first. When you give to others, you are giving with your full heart and without resentment. You are someone I'm proud to be a part of.

One of your most beautiful traits is how you let life flow, no matter what the challenge. You trust that it will all work out because you keep doing the best you can in each step of the process. You take care of yourself when times are tough, instead of tearing yourself down. You treat yourself as though you are dealing with your best friend. You are encouraging, compassionate, and loving, while facing your challenges along the way. You know you are learning some kind of lesson, so you do whatever you need to do in order to stay open on every step of the journey. You are AMAZING! I love you!

With Love and Gratitude,
An Empowered Woman

THE FEELING OF A HEALTHY AND LOVING RELATIONSHIP...

Dear Partner.

Thank you for being in my life. You are truly amazing. You show me love in so many different ways. You listen to my thoughts and feelings about life and you are there with encouraging words when I stumble. You are so great at staying positive with me. Even when I'm upset or struggling, you are a positive force of love. You give me space to be where I am, and you are there when I'm ready to talk and process whatever I'm going through.

I love how much we trust each other. I know we are best friends and that we have a mutual respect. We cherish, honor, and are loyal to our relationship. We live and let live. I love and accept you as you are, and you do the same for me. We communicate with open hearts and listening ears. We grow together in our love and compassion for the world.

I love you so much. I love that we respect each other's different ways of thinking. There is no *one* right way. We are different, yet we find wonderful connections. We can each look at the other's viewpoint and be able to express how it works or doesn't in our own lives. I feel gratitude in every part of me for getting to enjoy you in my life. I don't know how long you will be on this journey with me, but I know you will be here for as long as you are supposed to be.

With Love and Gratitude,

A Loving Me

BECOMING WHAT WE STAND FOR...

Dear Women's Empowerment

(or whatever cause you feel passionate about),

I see women as a beautiful source of balance in this world. Women are here to be cherished for all the traits they offer. I love seeing women who know their worth transforming the world. That is as authentic as we can get. When we know our worth and can present ourselves in a loving way, we show the world compassion. We are retraining society on how people should treat each other.

We've come so far since the days when we let rage lead us. We saw how the changes emanating from rage and anger didn't last. We see now that self-love is essential for creating *positive changes in the world*. Our light shines bright when we are serving humanity from a loving place. Men feel as though they are part of the change, instead of feeling like outsiders who must walk on eggshells. We are heard with open hearts and defenses down, instead of triggering the twelve-year-olds inside each other by using hate and ugliness to make points.

We see that it wasn't one sex that got us where we were; we all contributed. We are the change, redefining our roles. We understand that it takes time and a whole lot of patience. This process is about progress. I'm so happy that I learned to see life through clearer spectacles. I understand the challenges in changing my own individual feelings, thoughts, perspectives of truth, and actions. I can't expect others to do it any faster. We are *all* works in progress.

I love supporting women in finding their own inner voices, even if a woman's causes and beliefs are different from mine. What is important is that she sees her path for herself. We get that clear vision when we treat ourselves with the love and respect we deserve. That's why I love assisting women to find that respect and love for themselves. The most magical moment is when a woman starts being able to say, *I'm valuable and important and I deserve my own time.*

The internal light that goes on becomes so bright that their outer world starts shifting to embrace this new force. I love doing what I do. I approach women's empowerment from a loving place. When challenges come up, I go back and ask, *Am I handling this situation from a loving place?* If I'm not, I come up with different perspectives until I can get to a loving place. That's when I know the time is right to come up with solutions. I commit to the cause by representing myself in a loving way toward myself, community, nation, and world. Love guides my way.

With Love and Gratitude,

An Empowered Me

THE SHIFT

Once we've gotten to the point where we can see clear visions, our goals for what we want to see in ourselves and in our world create a shift. We start being presented with people and opportunities to either learn from or build the love inside us. Just in case you are one of those people doubting this, I can tell you that I was there. I'm a survivor of multiple traumas. I've been to the depths where I believed death was my only way to be free. I didn't just think about suicide, I attempted it. From that low point, I could see the ways my life didn't work. I couldn't change the people around me. I could only change how I chose to live my life. You can have the internal life you want. Once you find the key, the outer world will start responding in a way beyond your wildest dreams. Start with the steps listed in this book and watch yourself get stronger and clearer. This is a shift that comes from doing the work and aligning yourself with the positive energy that you want to see more of in your life and in the world. Trust the process.

When we shift, we start transforming the world without even knowing it; our energy goes way beyond our physical bodies, and what we put out into the world expands. We may notice people being nicer and treating us with more respect. We start noticing little ways we can contribute to the betterment of our relationships, communities, state, country, environment, and world. When we shift, transformations happen in the most authentic and genuine way. If you are anything like me, this will get you giddy when you start noticing. The process is magical.

RELATIONSHIP WITH DIVINE LOVE...

Dear Divine Source of Love,

Thank you for creating me in your image of *Divine Love*. I commit to focusing my attention on people who are representatives of the love I want to see in the world. You have given me many wonderful examples of people exuding love from their *being* (authentic self). There hasn't been any *one* religion, belief, or group that has shown the beauty of expressing love. *Every* group and *every* individual within a group has the ability to express and share love. I'm open to seeing *all* the love the world has to offer. I will honor the love I see. I commit myself to seeing the miracles that the power of love and compassion creates. Instead of worrying about what other people's beliefs are, I now focus on the bigger picture: how can I serve humanity through expressions of love?

Since my definition of you is *Divine Love*, I commit to keeping the definition of that love clear in my head at all times. If the definition is clear, I don't confuse my judgments, jealousy, envy, fear, anger, and righteousness with love. For I know that, any time I'm acting out of that space, I'm not operating from a loving place.

My clarity on the definition of *Divine Love* has set me free, but I only got there through the lessons you set before me to show me everything that love wasn't. What became most clear in my darkest times was the love I didn't have for myself. *I was acting against you by acting against me.* I didn't love myself, so I couldn't clearly see you. I didn't realize the path to you lay in honoring the person you created when you brought me here.

I commit to being the best person I can be. I will give and show love to myself so I can see clearly and maintain healthy boundaries. I will do my best to stay loving in the most turbulent settings, but I won't beat myself up if fear and confusion temporarily take over. I understand that when I abuse myself, I'm rejecting you. If I stay aware and awake in the moment I'm in, I am connected to you.

With Love and Gratitude,

An Empowered Me

DIVINE LOVE

The path to experiencing *Divine* Love is a miracle in itself. The more we spot it in the world, the more we have it inside. If we don't recognize it outside of ourselves, it's because the love for ourselves needs more clarifying. Self-love is the key to experiencing authentic love on a regular basis. Love becomes action when we are one with it. We act and see in a way that attracts amazing people and situations to our lives. We learn what it means to experience full and authentic abundance. The best part is that we see our relationship with the Divine clearly, no matter how we personally define it. This is the place where we learn to separate what we think we're supposed to believe from what our heart tells us. It's a true awakening.

We begin to see and question anything that doesn't represent love. For some, this piece is terrifying, but for others it is liberating. We get to let go of the fear and judgments of not being enough in the eyes of the Creator of the Universe, to realize that we deserve to give and receive *Divine Love* as much as anyone else does. We are worthy.

Our job isn't to judge other religions as better or worse, good or bad, but to see where the love is and celebrate the loving energy in *all beings*. When we experience love, we are experiencing the greatest gift of all. What some may not realize is that we have the capability of seeing and spotting this love every day. The empowered woman knows how to love both internally and externally. When we are close to our *Source*, the love becomes stronger and clearer. We are tapping into the energy of the Universe, the same energy that the power of prayer comes from. When our prayers are fueled by love, we become unstoppable.

GOING DEEPER

Spot Loving Acts. We get more of what we focus on, right? Instead of spending time judging others, try to find and focus on spotting and sharing loving acts of kindness. What messages can you find in the news and on social media that represent your definition of love? You can spot them in banks, shopping, on social media, TV, and in print. There are tons of sites dedicated to loving acts of kindness. Share that on social media.

FILLING INNER DARKNESS WITH LOVE...

Dear Inner Darkness,

I see you. You are run by all my fears. I know how to spot you leaking out into the world. When I start reading and participating in gossip, I'm feeding you. If I start attracting toxic people to my life, I am getting ready to learn from you. When I have unforeseen challenges come up, I see my *choice* in feeding you or embracing you with my love. I always have the *choice*. By seeing you, I take away your power over me. I'm not ashamed of you being in my life, because you have so much to teach me. I'm also not ashamed to be me. I have made choices in my life that have also been learning opportunities. I've learned the lessons I was meant to learn, so my past is healed. Love is in control now.

I can feel you stir when times are tough. I can hear your voice calling me when I'm triggered by others' beliefs and actions. I choose to keep my ear tuned to love. I know I have to change the old beliefs that don't serve the life I have now. You actually help me because, every time I'm triggered emotionally by someone else's actions, you peek your head out to see whether I've healed or I still have work to do. Seeing you clearly helps me realize that I have a *choice*. I can see through your eyes of fear and stay in the world of problems and victimhood, or I can see through the eyes of love and find solutions and heroes.

I can choose to see that I'm not the victim of other people's actions, but the hero of my own reactions. I don't have to match any toxic person's fearful energy. No matter what happens in my life, I'm never without choice on how to guide my feelings, thoughts, and actions.

This doesn't mean I won't choose you at times; I know I will. Sometimes I may get to the point where I forget that I have choices and do not have the energy to pull myself up. This isn't the time to wallow. What I once believed was rock bottom, I now know is the path to breakthrough. When I have a breakthrough, I grow stronger by releasing my toxic energy through tears, movement, and transformative thinking. I'm not scared of you anymore. In the darkness I see what is blocking my light from reaching deeper and stretching out farther. I don't have to take out my pain on anyone else. My old beliefs are transformed into healing perspectives when I embrace you with the light of love. Thank you for all the lessons I get from being open enough to see you.

With Love and Gratitude,

An Empowered Me

EMBRACING OUR DARKNESS

Our darkness can be one of our greatest teachers. Think back to Part I of this book. What did you see and feel within yourself during that section? For many, it may have triggered some serious darkness. We don't have to look back and judge that. If we learn from it, the purpose of being there has been served. If we start spotting the darkness when it's happening, we are shifting away from letting it lead our lives. The darkness will be there anytime we want or need to tap into it.

Living in fear is being trapped in a fearful perspective of reality. If we don't want to be there, we need to change our perspectives to loving ones. Some may argue with you and fight for their fearful thinking. They may use their *beliefs* to attack. Their beliefs are perspectives, the same as anything we want to believe. If it makes you happy, keeps you functioning, brings on positive change in your life and the lives of others, *do you really care if someone's fearful beliefs agree with yours or not?*

Embracing the empowered woman within us is looking our own darkness in the eyes and appreciating the lessons that come from it without needing to feel shame for having it. We can see the value in our darkness without choosing to let it run our lives. When we see our own darkness, we can see when other people are living in theirs. We see them with eyes of compassion. We can be grateful for what we learn from them. We can see other ways of viewing their dark actions. Instead of feeding on the fear that the darkness around us creates (terrorist attacks, school shootings, and mass shootings), we can focus on the compassion and love it brings out in others. There lies the real strength and power of what happens. We get to practice choosing fear or love, darkness or light, *every single day.* In this moment, which do you choose?

GOING DEEPER

Change your language. Look at your beliefs as perspectives. Instead of judging someone who is doing things differently from you, challenge yourself to go through more positive perspectives of thought. Work on observing and responding without attaching to a belief. Focus on what their perspective can teach you. It doesn't mean you have to go along with it, but you will be more open to hear and feel where they are coming from. If you see that it's a fearful perspective, pay attention to what comes up in you. Make observations without telling the person they are right or wrong.

SOLIDIFYING YOUR RELATIONSHIP WITH THE EMPOWERED WOMAN WITHIN...

To the Empowered Woman Within Me,

I see your strength, beauty, and wisdom clearly. I see who you are and what you stand for. Most of all, I see that I got here on my own accord. I had to be ready to accept and look at you. People gave me seeds along the way, but I had to make the choice to plant and grow them. I also had to determine which were weeds, and I had to take those out of my garden. Nobody can do that but me. It made me realize that I can't force others to do and be who I want them to be. That is not showing my empowerment.

I have to support people in discovering their own path. Their perspectives and beliefs can be different from mine, but I know if I support them on their journeys, we will have the ability to feel connected through love, joy, pain, and fear. We are *all* having a human experience. We *all* feel. When I'm not judging others as right or wrong, I can hear and listen to the feelings that are coming up. I can tell if they are beating themselves up like I used to do. I can see when shame and guilt are running their lives, and I can share my wisdom, perseverance, and hope of how I made it out. I am not responsible for successes or failures in someone else's life. That is their story and not mine to take responsibility or credit for. I didn't change and find you because someone *forced* me to.

First, I had to stop defining myself through my titles and other people's views of me. Then, when I was stripped down to feeling like I didn't exist, I had to figure out what mattered to me. This piece was a solo mission. I couldn't depend on my loved ones to help define me. I needed to work on what I believed about myself without things being skewed by outside opinion. My wanting to *always* please others is what kept me from serving in love.

To become you, I had to actualize a sense of love, compassion, and empathy toward myself that I wasn't ready for until I hit the moment of *awe*...the *awakening*. That *awe* moment wasn't forced, and it didn't happen until *I was ready to accept and love me*. Once I got it, I committed to bringing out my light.

When I am at one, when I feel peace instead of chaos, and when I tap into the love within in me, I make choices and see people in a compassionate and loving way. Even if I don't want the person in my life, I'm making the choice because it is what is best for my peace. They are on their own journey.

The most powerful thing I noticed in my transformation was that we are all magnets. I attract like energies. If I'm in a dark place, I'm going to attract dark energies. If I listen and watch, I will hear and see what I have to work on. If I'm in a place of love and light, I attract the most beautiful force field of light around me. People who want to bring out darkness in me can't get in. Most stay far away and, in fact, don't like me at all. That's fine with me! I realize that if I had like (dark) energy, he or she would feel pulled toward me. In those moments, I thank God for protecting me from energy that is unhealthy for me. I know the people I do attract are meant to be in my life. They are either showing me how to make my light brighter and extend my love outward, or they are showing me dark spots I need to work on.

I know that I don't want to be a part of assisting a person in beating her- or himself up. I want to support them in finding the love they have for themselves. When I do that, I feel great, and their drama doesn't have a negative effect on me.

My story is my own to create. I'm the only one who has my exact mix of character traits and circumstances. I get to choose my responses and my perspectives on what happens in my life. I can choose to see myself as heroine, victim, or villain. I *choose* what characters belong in my story for a chapter. I also choose how much play time they get throughout. Even if they choose not to be in my story in a physical sense, I still *choose* whether to keep them in my mind.

The best part of it all is that I can change my story. That is the superpower you gave me. I can choose different perspectives, and the whole story can take a turn. I can't change other people. The only person I can change is me. Being one with the empowered woman within me makes that a beautiful experience of strength, growth, love, respect, and compassion.

With Emanating Love and Gratitude,

A Much Better Me

COMMITTING TO THE EMPOWERED WOMAN WITHIN

None of us are perfect. No matter how far we get, there will be times when our darkness dims our light. It's what we do in those moments that shows us what we still need to work on and how far we have come. We are on this Earth for the exact time we are meant to be here. Some may not even take a breath of air before their lessons and mission for this life are done. Others will live over a hundred years because there are things to learn and to teach. They may be angry and bitter people, or loving and compassionate people. They are here for a purpose that is not ours to judge.

We get to make choices about what we want to represent in our lives. When we live consciously by defining who we are and what we stand for, we get a clear picture:

- We know where we want our energy to go.
- We are able to say *no* with firm and loving boundaries.
- We are able to say *yes* without feeling used and walked on.
- We understand ourselves and our choices, so we don't feel obligated to rationalize our decisions.
- We know when opportunities feel right and when they don't.
- We honor our feelings, thoughts, perspectives of truth, actions, responses, and intuitions.
- We empower ourselves to be the woman the world deserves—our authentic selves.

When we embrace the empowered woman within, we don't expect people to be anyone other than who we they are. If who they are doesn't work in our lives, we let them go. If they must stay in our lives, we figure out how to lovingly detach. We don't have to take how they live or what they say personally. We find solutions to dealing with them by being present and keeping our focus on what we *do* want. This is the power of self-care and being an empowered woman. When we do this, we transform the world by transforming ourselves. We take the power away from darkness in humanity and contribute only to the light.

What we *are* in charge of is how we treat ourselves and the people who come into our lives. Our stories don't have to be about what others do to us. That's our choice to make our stories about them. We get the opportunity to write ourselves the way we want to be written. Things that hurt us (betrayal, judgment, abuse, oppression) can create serious growth opportunities. What some may have considered the worst things that happened to me were actually my biggest eye-openers. Those "bad" events launched me into creating the life I have now—I *love* my life. I couldn't imagine a greater gift than to love the life we are given—lessons, blessings, and all.

GOING DEEPER

Evaluate the causes you serve. If the cause you support has lost its focus on what it stands for and replaced it with what it is against:

- How do you bring light into it?

- In what ways is the cause striking up defensive walls?

- Is it because it's using fear, manipulation, guilt, or shame as a catalyst for change?

- What is the end result the cause is looking to achieve?

- Is that a change in the world that inspires more love or more fear?

- If the answer is love, how do you inspire people without using fear-based methods?

- Is the cause inclusive? Here's an example: I support women's empowerment. By supporting women in loving and taking care of themselves, women become more authentic. We say no when we mean no and yes when we mean yes. We become better communicators in all facets of our lives. We become better partners, bosses, employees, lovers, friends, sisters, mothers, teachers, and students. When we change, so do men. They don't have to respond defensively because we aren't attacking. They do things to contribute to our empowerment because we are not trying to disempower them, and we notice more because we are not living in fear—*very* inclusive! We rise together!

Chapter 8

RIGHT HERE, RIGHT NOW!

FOR THE EMPOWERED WOMAN COMMITTING TO BE A BETTER ME.:.

Dear Me,

Thank you for honoring me by feeding me foods that make my body *feel* its best. Thank you for taking the time to slow down and meditate. Thank you for *creating* time to take care of me. I am full and abundant. Now that I've shown you how much I love you, I'm ready to support others. Today, I will be present when I'm running errands and working, so that I can smile and let my light shine toward anyone who may need a little extra. I will keep my focus on love to ensure that my conversations with people support them in coming up with the solutions that are best for them on their path. I commit to being aware of my darkness triggers as I listen to the news, scan social media, and face challenging situations.

I'm committing to be the best version of myself today. This does not mean I'm expecting to be perfect. I'm going to do my best and learn in the areas I need to. This will make me a better me. I'm committing to be me! Today, I will remember the words of my mother, who reminds me, *"It is none of your business what other people think of you."* It matters what *I* think of me and what I choose to do with my feelings, thoughts, actions, and beliefs toward others. Today, I'm choosing to show my love.

With Love and Gratitude,
An Empowered Woman

THE IMPORTANCE OF PRESENCE

Living in the moment we are in is the foundation of all solid structure. If we aren't where our feet are, our minds are unconscious of the moment we are living in. The more unconscious we are in the moment, the more we will perceive life as happening to us and not for us. We choose unconsciousness when we are living in the past, in the future, or in someone else's life. When we are anywhere but right here, our thoughts can be skewed. When we can see what's important in the moment, we come up with a plan for our day in that present space. Our daily activity becomes meaningful. Waking peaceful and present is better than starting the day jarred by the alarm bell, our minds instantly going to our to-do lists, and the stress that comes with the fear of lack of time.

FINDING OUR CENTER...

Dear Self,

Today, I'm centering myself in my daily activities. Each moment of my life counts, and I don't want to miss it. Just taking one activity at a time expands my awareness and enjoyment of the present moment.

As I lie in my bed, I feel my body as it adjusts to being awake. I slowly stretch my legs and my toes, feeling my body's energy beginning to flow. I stretch my arms as far as they will go, then release. As I put my feet on the ground, I feel the sensation of carpet under my toes. As I take a deep breath in, I feel my lungs fill and expand. I let go of my breath in a count of five, four, three, two, one.

I walk into the bathroom and look deeply into the eyes of the woman looking back at me. I love the woman staring back at me. As I brush my teeth, I feel the cool water as the bubbles fill my mouth. The soft bristles flow across my mouth and the essence of mint is felt with a tingle.

I wash my hands, taking deep breaths in and out as I absorb the smell of lavender as the lather builds. My hands feel tender and soft before I let the warm water rinse off each bubble. I put my hands up to my mouth and take a deep breath in. *Clean!* I'm ready for my day to begin.

With Love and Gratitude,

A Better Me

CENTERING

Centering ourselves first is essential for being peaceful within our own psyche. If we don't center ourselves, we can go into instant autopilot. I've been guilty of saying, "*I don't have enough time to...*" (whatever I could be doing better for myself). Centering ourselves with what we already do daily is a great start. We can start with a stretch where we focus on how our body feels as we reach up to the sky and lunge from side to side. We can practice gratitude in the mirror as we get ready for our day. While eating, we can slow down and pay attention to the food in our mouths. We choose the food we do for a reason. Take the time to taste it. We can use our senses to feel the sensations and textures. Taste the food moving around in your mouth and going into your body. Judgments about food and feelings of guilt, shame, or obligation are not in the present moment. We have to be present to enjoy what we are putting into our mouths.

Do you have a dog? Here's a great opportunity to become centered. While you're walking the dog, look around, look up, and look down. Listen to nature and note:

- What do you see and hear?
- Are there birds?
- Is there wind? Tune into the breeze.
- Where do you feel it?
- How does it feel?
- Is it cool or warm?
- If it's raining, what does that feel like against your skin?

When we are present and centered, we instinctually know what our bodies are asking for. The relationship to nurturing the body becomes peaceful, and it all starts with simply being conscious and present. The more centered we are, the more we want to do what is best for ourselves. It is natural and not forced. When we are forcing ourselves to do what is best for our self-care, we are stuck in internal wars—creating violence from within. We are fighting or feeling deprived. When we stop fighting and start loving, we end the war. When we end the war, our bodies stop responding as though we are attacking them.

GOING DEEPER

Center yourself in your daily activities. Practice being present while getting ready in the morning, doing dishes, making meals, going to the bathroom, eating food, drinking beverages, walking the dog, feeding the cat, walking, shopping, being with loved ones, cleaning, fixing, gardening, and any other thing you do during the day. Any time you think to center yourself, take a few deep breaths and just practice being right where your feet are. Use all your senses. They will keep you present!

Notice the following:

- How does your body feel?

- What textures and sensations do you notice?

- How does it taste?

- What are you seeing?

- What sounds do you hear?

- How does it smell?

Experience the moment you are in right here, right now. We have to get away from all the thoughts of future and past that are stressful and just *be in the moment*. How we do that is simply by noticing where our feet are and paying attention to anything that is within our sightline.

READY TO MEDITATE...

Dear Universe,

I used to be so intimidated by meditation. I've tried group meditations, silent meditations, chanting meditations, guided meditations, walking meditations, movement meditations, and sweat-covered meditations. I used to believe there was a right and wrong way to meditate. Then someone finally freed me from the beliefs that held me back. I discovered that, if I can breathe, I can meditate.

Now, I pay attention to my breath. Each time I'm focusing on my breath, I notice how much each inhale and exhale matters. Without breathing, I wouldn't exist. Appreciating the air moving through my body feels much more important when I take the time to think about it.

Inhaling to the count of ten, I feel and see my lungs expanding. Tingling sensations fill my nostrils as the air moves through me. I slowly exhale to the count of ten. I keep this breathing going as I imagine a white light cleansing my body, moving through me like a smooth flowing river would. I start at the crown of my head and go on until I've felt the energy flowing all the way down to my toes.

Once I've done this, I ask my question to you. Sometimes answers comes to me instantly through images I see. Other times, the presence I bring out of my mediation leads me to the answer. I'm always amazed at how, when I remain open, so do new pathways in my life. The answer may not come in a way I expect, but more clarity is there the clearer I am.

I now see meditation as a gift of clarity, peace, space, and answers. Thank you, Universe.

With Love and Gratitude,

A Better Me

MEDITATION

Okay, some of us love and others dread the thought of meditation. If you think you can't meditate, you're wrong. When we are conscious of our breath and present in our space, even for a mere twenty seconds, we are meditating. That is a simple ten-count inhale and a ten-count exhale. You can do that on the toilet—and, by the way, that's a great place to start your practice.

The answers to our prayers are often found in meditation. This doesn't mean the answers will be clear and straightforward. What it does mean is that we may be given a clear mind to know the next best step for the moment. If we truly trust in the universal power of attraction, Source, God, Divine Love, whatever that is for us, we have to remember that we only have the perspective of looking through a straw when the picture of our lives is the size of a piece of paper. Whatever little bit we choose to focus on, we feed on. If we don't trust that we are being guided by something bigger, we get lost in the chaos of the unknown. If we are open, and we can live in the moment, we win. Building the meditation muscle will help us see and hear the signs that are leading us. Even in our darkness, there is a space of clarity. Meditation helps us tap into that space.

Remember, meditation looks different for everybody. There are countless forms and practices. Whichever form of meditation works for you, use it until it doesn't work for you anymore, and then find another way. Don't do meditation because you think it's what you *should* be doing. Once again, *should* is a negative force, even if you are trying to do something positive. *Should* attaches to guilt and shame so that, if you don't do it, you can use it as a tool to beat yourself up. When you are ready, you will feel right about what you do and how you do it. That is why I give the examples of the toilet, eating, dog walking, and so on. Any of those can become meditation, and they come with a lot less pressure. There are plenty of movement practices that can be a form of meditation, like yoga, tai chi, and qi gong. As we treat ourselves better and better, we begin to take better care of ourselves. Meditation is a decision to bring peace and space into our minds and thoughts. It is a part of feeling whole.

GOING DEEPER

Meditate. You may choose silence, music, guided, or chanting. Don't judge the moment, just enjoy and be at one with your breath. Be at one with where you are. Don't worry about pushing thoughts away. Try watching them floating away like balloons. Start small and build your meditation muscle. Remember that you are exactly where you are supposed to be.

BECOMING ONE WITH SIMPLY BEING...

Dear Universe,

As I take in a deep breath, I feel the air moving through and filling me. I feel the blood within me openly flowing because of the oxygen permeating each cell in my body. I feel a tingling in my fingers and a profound energy surrounding and protecting me. My heaviness is transcended. I feel as if there is no body. My energy is bigger than the body that is containing it. With a focus on love, I see a bright light and become one with it as it permeates into everything around it. My life is open to you, Universe. Please help me see my next step on my path clearly. Lead me to the place that is best for me. Allow me to trust in the people and places I'm brought to. Let me be open to the possibilities of each moment. I know in this moment that I'm exactly where I'm supposed to be. In this moment, I'm not in need of anything other than what I have. In this moment, I'm complete. I'm here. *I AM.*

With Love and Gratitude,

A Better Me

BEING I AM

We can help ourselves stay present by being in the place of *I AM*. See I AM as a complete sentence about who you are. I know it's really tempting to want to add to it, but for this moment, I AM is enough. In the present moment, I AM is all we ever need to be. When we try to make it more than that, we load up expectations, obligations, guilt, shame, disappointment, and judgments if we can't live up to the extended version of the sentence, I AM. When we can detach from the titles that come after (such as mom, sister, wife, daughter, Republican, Democrat, Liberal, Conservative, employee, boss, victim, hero, single mom, Christian, Jewish, Muslim, employed, unemployed, pretty, ugly, love, hate, fear, joy, smart, stupid, homeless, rich, or poor), we can accept ourselves, knowing that simply *being* and existing is enough.

This practice releases us from some of our toxic triggers that come with the definition of any of those things. If we are not being what we think we *should* be because of a title, we trigger our fears. No matter which of those titles is taken away, we still exist. Even if we are not acting from a loving place, we still matter. Even if we don't have a job, house, husband/wife, or money—we still matter. Our purpose in living isn't gone because we aren't attached to a title.

Without all those titles, who are we? Break it down all the way to the very core: I AM. This doesn't mean that those aspects of ourselves aren't a part of our journey. When we can be in I AM, we simply take the pressure off ourselves to be anything more than we are in this exact moment. It stops limiting us. When we stop focusing on our own sense of obligation, guilt, judgment, and shame, we stop focusing on *others'* obligations, guilt, judgment and shame. We stop focusing on their titles. We stop expecting others to fit titles we are defining for them. Our attachment to titles can bring us together or tear us apart. By practicing I AM, we see the truth in it for all of us. We see our Divine right to be.

If we can practice being in this space, even for a short time each day, we get to feel complete peace in just *being*. When we can do that, we become more open to seeing ourselves and others without walls. Here is where we can listen and be open to solutions that are truly in the best interests of the people involved.

None of us have a perfect thinking mind. If we did, there would be no war within ourselves and no war with others. As we go into I AM, we stop blaming ourselves and others. We see that blame isn't who we are. It is the war we have within us. We don't have to get defensive with others when we know who we are without any titles.

GOING DEEPER

Be in the space of I AM. Take a deep breath and release it fully, until all the breath has been pushed out of you. Be still for a moment. Repeat "I AM" in a chant through each breath. Be one with the statement. If you feel a title coming up, recognize that is not who *you* are. You are complete right here and right now.

FOR THE EMPOWERED WOMAN READY TO SERVE...

Dear Divine,

Please show me where you want me to be. I see places in
the world that need compassion, love, and peace. What
is my part? Is it spreading love and compassion on social
media? Is it traveling to some of these areas that are
struggling? Is it helping my community by showing up at
meetings? Is it donating time or money? Is it being the
example of love in my home for my children and partner?
Is it creating a home for someone who doesn't have one?
If you give me a sign, I will show up! What can I do right
now to help transform the world?

With Love and Gratitude,

A Better Me

DIVINE TIMING

Divine timing means that everything happens exactly in
the time it is supposed to happen and there is a reason for
everything happening the way it does. There are no accidents.
We are exactly where we are supposed to be in every given
moment. Think about this for a second—if we are present
and believe in Divine timing, the should-haves, could-haves,
and would-haves don't exist. They are not real and they have
no power. Without judging ourselves and others, we create a
place of peace inside us. We are given daily opportunities to
contribute to the world. Anytime we participate in a loving act
of kindness, we are helping the world. If we stay present, we
see opportunities. Divine timing is a perspective of thought.

We each get to decide how to view the events in our and other people's lives. Divine timing is not stressful. It takes the unnecessary suffering out of our experience.

Here's an example: *A woman is sitting in church. She is completely absorbed in what is happening in the moment. A mission is there to discuss the work they are doing in a foreign country. The woman feels this cosmic pull to sign up. She starts looking into going, and everything lines up in her favor to go. Now, it might not look like this if she weren't present. In fact, to the outside world, it appears that her life is falling apart. Her boss told her they were dissolving her position. Her husband left her for another woman. Divine timing cleared her plate so she was free to go. If she weren't present and open, she might have seen these events as catastrophic, even as punishments. Being present allowed her to see that following her cosmic urge is now opening up her life and heart to helping people in a foreign country. When we, in the outside world, aren't present, we might feel sorry for her because we are caught up in our own egos' ideas of what we think her life should look like. In reality, she's exactly where she is supposed to be.*

One of the biggest blessings I see in those times of darkness is the love and compassion of others. Think about natural disasters, terrorist attacks, school shootings, and abuse cases. We get to live the experience our mind creates. If I believe in Divine timing, I can pull meaning from the madness. I can be a part of the healing process. If I go into a dark place, and don't believe in Divine timing, I can go to war both internally and externally. I can get stuck judging everything and everyone as not enough. A belief is our perspective of truth.

Even reading this book and this page is happening in Divine timing. Money shows up, people show up, animals show up, nature shows up. Divine timing reminds us that we are exactly where we are supposed to be. We can serve from any moment we are in; we just need to be open.

GOING DEEPER

Choosing perspectives of truth. When choosing what to believe and what not to believe, we have to ask ourselves:

- Are these beliefs serving me?
- Are these beliefs serving my community?
- Do these beliefs deplete me or give me energy?
- Do these perspectives of truth create more love or more fear?

SERVING FROM A LOVING PLACE TODAY...

Dear Self,

My focus is on me and where I'm letting my energy go today. My energy will be put out there to serve in the best interest of my community today. I will carefully watch my thinking to see how I can best serve my neighbors. I will refrain from judging them or myself in a fear-filled manner.

These are the questions I will ask myself:

- Are my thoughts loving ones?
- Am I showing compassion?
- Am I practicing loving acts with myself and others?

By serving you the best I can, I serve my community from the strongest and most loving place possible. Today, I'm serving with love and transforming the world.

With Love and Gratitude,

A Better Me

SERVING OTHERS

When we are serving with love, no matter how people respond to us, we feel complete. Our worth was there before we served. To serve with love is powerful and energizing and exists only in the present moment. We serve from love when we feel the call (in the present moment) to serve in the name of love. There are no expectations of what we will get back when we serve from here. Since many of us are still working through our old beliefs, it takes a great deal of presence to be authentic in where we are serving—love and abundance or fear and lack.

When we authentically serve our communities with love, solutions look and feel quite different. We stop feeling like our way is the only way. We open up to hear others and add to our thinking, instead of being at war with others who are doing the best they can to serve. When we speak from a loving place, others are less prone to feel attacked. It helps to keep communication open. How do we know when we've reached each other's fear triggers? We get defensive.

We don't have to defend love. If we feel as though we do, we may have to revisit our definition of love. People are going to react to us based on where they are. Not everyone is going to like you when you are serving from a loving place. If people hate themselves, they are not capable of loving you. They can only show you what they have inside. This doesn't mean they won't agree with you and try to make you happy.

Sometimes we are called to serve in some challenging situations. A friend in an abusive situation calls on us; we are first responders to a terrorist attack; we are protecting children during a school shooting; we are supporting a child who has experienced trauma; we are serving a country where there is a lack of clean water. We still have the choice to serve out of fear or love. Choosing love takes a great deal of presence during every second. We can go from love to fear easily under these traumatic conditions. We simply need to remain open and accept where we are in each moment.

If I'm serving with love, I'm not attached to the end game. I'm right here in the moment, supporting the person through the traumatic event. Righteousness is *not* love. Being there with compassion, no matter what that person is experiencing, is love. If you are the one there, you are the one who is meant to be there. If you are not there, you are not meant to be there. There are no accidents; you are where you are supposed to be. Serving with love is the only way we can even begin to transform the world to be better. We have to show love to create more of it. Likewise, if we serve with fear, we are only creating more of it. Becoming the empowered woman transforms the world.

GOING DEEPER

Exploring our ability to serve from a loving place.
Get out your definition of love from the Chapter 7 "Define Love" exercise. In times of chaos, you will want to have this available on a regular basis. Ask the Universe, Source, and/or yourself:

- How I can serve the situation with love?

- How do I face hate with love when the hate is striking so much fear in our society?

Explore your feelings, thoughts, and perspectives of truth to make sure they are aligned with serving from a loving place:

- Are my feelings contributing to the hate?

- Am I engaging in hate-filled feelings, thoughts, or perspectives of truth?

- What perspectives of truth am I engaging in to serve with love?

- How do I convert my fearful beliefs into loving beliefs?

- Do I feel like I'm better than or less than another person?

- How do I feel when I'm serving my loving beliefs?

Pay attention to your growth in your answers. Celebrate the progress.

Chapter 9

TRANSFORMING THE WORLD

THE EMPOWERED WOMAN WITHIN...

To the Empowered Woman Within Me,

I'm beyond happy to see you! I know you have been within me all along. Your strength, spirit, wisdom, beauty, and courage have permeated every part of me now. I can hear your voice inside me. I feel myself striving and growing on a regular basis. You are not just within me now but, because you have brightened the light within me, I can share you with the world around me. I can bring you into every relationship and every situation I'm brought into.

I can trust that I am exactly where I'm supposed to be, and I have the tools to work through any lesson that is brought to me. I'm open to seeing the blessings that come from being one with you. Thank you for helping me see the power within me. Your loving nature helps me see that any lesson I'm going through is essential to making you stronger, so I don't have to be hard on myself when I am put in situations where there is a learning curve. I enjoy the learning process now, instead of worrying about what I'm going to mess up and what I did wrong. I get that life is trial and error and, the more loving I am, the more I will learn to trust that staying present is the key to achieving my goals to let you shine in the world.

Thank you for helping me see I'm worthy. I'm here with purpose, and my love is the guide that will take me through this life with peace and grace. I'm so grateful that now, when I look in the mirror, I see you.

With Love and Gratitude,
The Empowered Woman

CONNECTING TO THE EMPOWERED WOMAN WITHIN

Connecting to our own empowered woman is just like any other relationship. How you treat her will dictate how the relationship goes. By keeping up with the practices suggested in this book, you will get the tools to nurture your relationship with her. If you choose to do nothing to support her, she will weaken. The passion that drives you into action will fizzle. You will go back into wanting and lacking modes instead of being in positive action modes. Keep your connection strong! Vision boards are a great way to keep her in full view. I took an old desk calendar and used a ton of magazines to find quotes, words, and phrases that reminded me of the person I'm committing myself to being. Every time I'm writing at my desk, I see her. I draw strength and courage to be the most authentic version of me that I'm capable of being in this moment. I consciously take time to look at my board on a regular basis.

Letters are another great way to connect with her. When we can write from the heart and let the words take on a whole new life, we can be brought to tears by the power of the connection. We create contracts with her to encourage her to shine. That can also happen during meditation. Connecting to her is connecting to the abundance of love we have within us.

We connect to our empowered woman any time we choose to live from a loving place. Fear holds us hostage and love sets us free. This is true in our internal world and it is true in our external world. Now that you truly know the meaning of love, hopefully you can see where there is proof of this in your own life.

The empowered woman doesn't need to attack unless the situation she is put in requires physical action to remove herself. If we stay present, we stay clear on what the moment requires of us. If we get in our head and get into defense mode when the moment doesn't require it, we aren't available to be there and be open to hear ideas and perspectives other than the wounded girl within us. Connect to the empowered woman, and we show the world why we are essential.

GOING DEEPER

Bringing the empowered woman with you everywhere you go. Ask yourself:

- How would she react when someone crossed a personal boundary?
- Would she dropkick the person, adding to the violence, or would she be clear and firm about her boundaries?

If the boundaries continue to be pushed:

- Does she stay present and take the next step in making her boundaries clear (e.g., going above the person she is dealing with)?
- Does she remember that the person she is dealing with is hurting and offending her because of what is inside them?

When she makes a statement:

- Does she attack or stay true to herself and enter the situation from a loving place?
- Is she present with the positive change she wants to create?
- Is she serving the betterment of humanity by the message she is spreading?

MAKING FRIENDS WITH LIFE...

Dear Life,

I love you! I love you! I love you! Thank you for giving me the air every morning to breathe in what you are offering me. Thank you for giving me the opportunity to live this day to the best of my ability. I know you don't expect me to do any better or any worse than whatever I do today. I know that, whatever my choices are, I will learn from them. Thank you for working with me as I learn to be the best version of me that I can be.

I had a rough start. When I was young, I treated you as my enemy. That thought pattern caused a lot of pain in my life. Yet, now, I feel so much love around what were once very traumatic experiences. I see how those experiences gave me a place available for compassion, empathy, and wisdom that is essential to giving back to the world. I see how my thoughts around my past created chaos in my life, and so, all the lessons I was given seemed more challenging. As I've grown in my love for you, I've seen the direct correlation in the love I had for me. The more I love me, the more I get to love you. The more I love you, the more love I have the opportunity to contribute to the world.

Loving you supports me in not beating myself up. Loving you keeps me open. When I get into my dark place, I feel the love for you turn to fear. The difference is that now I have tools to get me out of that place. I love and accept you for exactly what you are.

With Love and Gratitude,
The Empowered Woman

MAKING LIFE OUR FRIEND

Making life our friend gives us so many wonderful opportunities to live, love, grow, and expand. Life is our friend when we stop fighting what is going on. We've come to acceptance that there is something to learn from everything that is going on in our own lives and in the world. We stop separating ourselves, and we start engaging in our lives. We stop saying *I can't do this* and start working on *how* to do it. This is what gives us the power to transform the world. We don't have the need to numb ourselves to avoid life, which releases us from our toxic addictions. Fear of the unknown future becomes unnecessary. When we stay present and love life, our focus becomes how to make a better life today. We don't have to use fear agendas or manipulative calls for action.

Fear lives in our attachment to the past and the future. Remember that chapter on gratitude? If we can focus on the blessings of each day, we see how much a positive vision of today can change lives. This doesn't mean we don't set goals for the future of our lives and the lives of generations to come. Goal-setting gives us a vision and supports us in coming up with daily actions to reach the goal we are looking to achieve. Knowing your own personal mission statement can also be a great way to create action steps toward your life goals. Just remember that, whatever happens in life, we can find meaning. If we choose to believe that, we will find the life lesson, no matter how painful the experience is. The lessons transform into blessings any time we learn from them. This is how we can remain a friend to life even if we get dealt some hard-hitting cards.

The empowered woman must embrace life as it is in order to create the changes to make it better. We have to be conscious of where are minds are. The life we create in our heads will be projected out into our realities. When we love our lives, our lives will love us back. What story are you feeding that goes against the love you want in your life? Only you are empowered to change the story.

GOING DEEPER

Create a mission statement. What is your own personal mission statement about how you want to serve humanity? If you need assistance, you can type "mission statements" into your search engine and see what comes up. Pull out your definition of love, then write your mission.

EMBRACING HUMANITY WITH LOVE...

Dear Humanity,

I love you. I believe that connecting to you with acts of love is the answer to a better life. I release myself from the fear that once was my guide. I will live guided by love. I don't have to have the same overall beliefs, the same colored skin, the same sexual orientation, the same politics, the same religion, the same ethnicity, and/or the same country as someone else. All I have to remember is that we all experience the same love, fear, joy, anger, happiness, and sadness. Each of us can tap into love or fear in any moment. I get the choice to live from a place of abundance or lack, no matter what my circumstances look like to anyone else. I'm free to make choices that will lead me to more love or more fear. I can choose to change when I feel the need to change. No one can force me to live in love or in fear.

I trust that whoever is brought into my life is a blessing. I will get the opportunity to learn and to teach. As long as I can remember to stay connected to love, I'm serving humanity to the best of my ability. I'm transforming the world! My worth isn't connected to another person's actions for better or worse. My worth is connected to simply being me. The more love and respect I show myself, the more I can give to my fellow human.

My love for humanity is not based on what I will get back. Love comes into my life because I'm open to seeing it. I'm open to seeing it because I recognize the love within myself. I only see what I believe I am inside. When I'm shining my inner light, I will not be faced with any darkness that isn't meant to teach something. I see that nobody is out to hurt me personally. Hurt people will attempt to hurt others. It is not about me, it's about them. If I get hurt by another person's darkness, the question becomes: what am I believing about myself in this moment?

A hate-filled person will spew out hate toward me. If I react to that hate with more hate, I already have that hate and rage inside me. Love-filled people will bring out the love in me. If the energies match up, the people who come in will stick around until the energies don't match anymore. People will serve their purpose in my life until their purpose in my life is complete. I trust that each person is in my life for the exact time that they are meant to be there. It is my job to represent the changes I *want* to see in the world and not contribute to the negative energy of the things I don't want to see.

With Love and Gratitude,

The Empowered Woman

FALLING IN LOVE WITH HUMANITY

To best serve humanity, we must love humanity. We can't just love the people who love and agree with us. We aren't always going to like people's choices. Some people are out there doing some very hurtful things. A person who is stuck in their darkness projects toxic energy, whether they mean to or not. When we love humanity, our focus is on breaking the cycle. Our goal is illuminating the path to incontrovertible transformation. If we encourage shame and guilt when we are trying to create positive change, we are just continuing a cycle of violence.

When we encourage a person to feel bad about themselves for the decisions they make, we are perpetuating the fear cycle.

If you don't understand a person's actions, educate yourself. How? Ask questions. If you don't understand someone's religion, look at it from his or her view of the religion, not that of someone who doesn't believe in it. If you don't understand mental illness or addiction, educate yourself on mental illnesses or addictions. If you don't understand why or how a person voted the way they did, ask, without judgment or a sense of righteousness that you know better. Research it from the standpoint of someone who is opposite of you, and be open to listening to their experience with compassion. We are all individuals who are living our lives according to our own perspectives of truth.

When we see the fear cycle in action, we can ask ourselves, *what would I do if I only felt love in this situation?* If you are still new to this way of thinking, keep your definition of love nearby. Let's take dealing with a man who is demeaning to women. If we are reacting in fear, we may want to attack. Love might say, walk away. Let him know lovingly how what he says comes across to you. Ask him if that is what he means to do. When we don't take them personally, we are more likely to ask questions. If we feel ourselves stirring inside, the best choice may be to walk away. With space, we can find the nonviolent things to do. Sometimes that may be to not engage with this person at all. If a person is a narcissist, our words won't matter to them, so if we choose to say words to them, we say them for ourselves, out of our own self-love. Doing this will often drive narcissists away. They don't like engaging with people who don't blame or who won't give their power away. If dealing with a narcissist or sociopath, education is key to not taking their actions personally. If they already had an effect on your self-worth, showing yourself love is the cure.

To love humanity, we have to be open to understanding humanity. If we want to help humanity be better, we must find ways to communicate with people from a loving place of compassion. People hating themselves doesn't create positive change. By being empowered, we transform ourselves and the world. Empowerment creates positive change for everyone it touches.

CONNECTING WITH NATURE...

Dear Nature,

You are a great teacher about where I am in any given moment. If I'm not present, I don't pay attention to you at all, unless what you're doing has a direct effect on my safety or the safety of others. If I've slowed down my thoughts enough to see your beauty, I notice the formation of clouds, birds flying, trees moving, sounds filling the air, and the majestic way water moves. I notice your creations.

When I want to learn from you, I see how important it is to focus on where my feet are when facing your uneven ground (stay present). I understand when I look at water that it must keep flowing (being present and feeling through my struggles without resistance, a.k.a. addictions). Resisting only builds up pressure and creates more chaos.

I appreciate the life of a caterpillar (learning how to go from surviving to thriving). I see the purpose of the chrysalis (sitting in stillness and contemplation) to let the transformation take hold. I feel the power of the emerging butterfly (our inner strength, wisdom, and beauty are seen by the world). I can feel the energy (we are all energy) of a tree that is full of life. I watch how weeds (our negative thoughts) can damage the life of the plants, flowers, and trees that they steal energy from. Smothering vines take over and block the plant from receiving life-giving sunshine.

There are so many lessons you offer me. I'm grateful to be your student. Being one with you grounds me. Thank you for giving me the opportunity to slow down and get out of my own way.

With Love and Gratitude,

The Empowered Woman

EMBRACING NATURE AS A TOOL

Finding our own lessons from nature acts as a centering tool. It helps us get out of the human box that we sometimes create for ourselves. When we look at nature and how it works, it can help clear our vision and get out of our resistance to the changing tide. We are meant to change, grow, and expand. Our journey is meant to be transformational.

Nature is a great place to gain perspective, even if that means going right outside our door and planting our feet on the Earth. Take the time to feel the energy of the Earth come up through your toes. Use your senses and really feel the energy, smell the air, and hear whatever noises she brings you in that moment. Imagine yourself as a tree, with your roots extending through the Earth and stretching through each grain of dirt and speck of sand. Nature is a reminder that we are all connected energy.

When we connect through love, we create; when we connect through fear, we destroy.

Think about a raging river. We can see how the water moves despite anything in its way. If it can't get through one way, it will find another way, but it keeps flowing. Then, at times, it will come to a place where it runs slowly and peacefully before picking up speed again. It's just like life; we will hit bumps and certain doors will be closed so we can't get through, but it means we find another way. It may not be the path we thought would be best, but that's just our thinking. If a door is closed, there is always another way. Life will keep flowing and, if we don't resist it, we know we are going exactly where we are meant to be. There will be times where the water is peaceful and other times where we have to move with bursts of energy.

To live empowered is a daily practice, and we need all the tools we can get to keep us in a loving and empowered place. We are offered fear daily, but we don't have to accept it. Remember to connect with nature. When nature brings tornados, hurricanes, fires, floods, and tsunamis, we learn about love, compassion, empathy, change, rebuilding, community, priorities, and the value of life itself. Nature teaches *this too shall pass* and that we have no idea what tomorrow will bring. If that is not a good reason to live today, I don't know what is. Our judgments of good and bad are us looking at a straw-hole-sized part of the big picture. We have no idea why things happen the way they do. What we can do is keep learning, growing, and expanding.

When we start respecting nature and the lessons she has to offer, we begin transforming our beliefs, thoughts, and actions to take better care of her. We start being more conscious of how we can help sustain her beauty. We start standing up for survival in our own way. Just another way we transform the world by becoming empowered.

GOING DEEPER

Take a walk. Before you take the walk, ask the Universe a question about your life. Ask to receive the answer while you're walking. If you feel drawn to go to a particular place—go there! Walks are great for so many reasons, but the one we will focus on here is to stay in tune with nature. Look around and observe what you see. No phones allowed. You don't want to be distracted from getting the answer to your question. Pay close attention to the messages you see in nature. Trust what you observe on your walk and see what comes to you. What does what you see, hear, touch, feel, and/or taste represent to you? Your answers can be hidden in the details.

FUELING OUR SPIRITUALITY WITH LOVE...

To the Source of All Love and Light.

I believe in you. Every time I see you in the external world, I'm seeing you in me. You didn't make any mistakes in any of your creations. I know that each life serves a purpose. It's not my job to understand what your purpose is for everything you create. I know I'm meant to learn from the darkness that is in the world by embracing and embodying your light. You are the source of love that is bigger than any human comprehension.

I trust, when I pray, that you are answering my prayers. You give me signs of what to do next. If I'm meant to read a book, multiple people will bring up the book to me or I will feel drawn to it when I see it. If I am meant to meet someone, I listen to the gifts they offer me through our interaction. If I'm meant to assist in helping animals, nature, or humans, I'm led there by your call.

When I ask you how to show others love, I have to go deeper and go within. The way that is best for me to serve will come to me authentically. You gave me my unique features and skills for a reason. You made me who I am.

When it comes to our relationship, I trust the messages I feel. When I feel drawn to a church, I will be there. When I feel drawn to nature, I will be there. When I feel drawn to interactions with others, I will be there. When I feel the urge to read, I will read.

I choose to serve love. I choose to feed the love within myself. I choose to see all your offerings to my life as blessings. Thank you for showing me the way to experience you. You no longer are lost in my thoughts of what is real and what isn't. I will do my best to bring you into all my decisions. If I fall away from you, I will find my way back.

With Love and Gratitude,
The Empowered Woman

PUTTING LOVE INTO OUR SPIRITUALITY

I know spirituality and religion can be a touchy subject. We can get fixated on our beliefs, thinking that what we believe is the only truth. That is *our* choice—our perspective of truth. What is important is to know if our beliefs are causing us to live in love or in fear. If we live in fear in our spirituality, we spread fear into every aspect of our lives. We have the power to put love into any spiritual or religious practice we have. It is where *our* mind focuses that matters. We are all individuals. Even within the same practice, there will be different views and interpretations. If our practice supports us in spreading love (keep your definition of love close) to ourselves and others without bias, our practice will be at one with our empowered actions. We will contribute to transforming the world.

We may find that there are many similar beliefs and visions. How we use our practice to serve is what is important. When practicing an organized religion, pay close attention to what feels right and what doesn't. Remember that each person who serves their religion is doing the best they can, but they are interpreting a vision arising out of their own experiences. It is our job to look at our experiences in the context of what we believe. We live with purpose. We show our love to the world by embracing the journey as we love, grow, and learn in this classroom called life.

My spirituality includes seeing the love inside the people I encounter. I may find that their love is buried, and see that it's not healthy or safe to be in direct contact. I can pray that those people will one day find the love within themselves. I can hope that they begin to love themselves so that they stop spreading hate in the world. If they aren't ready for the help, they won't be helped. In those cases, prayer is my job, creating healthy boundaries is my job, and supporting the people whose lives have been affected might just be my job, but I only know what my job is by staying centered and connecting with Source. Trust *your* connection! The answer may just be enough to know the next step. With each step, more will be revealed.

GOING DEEPER

Finding love in our spirituality. When we are exploring spiritual concepts, we can look at how they fit into our lives through the foundation of love. Ask yourself:

- How has this worked in my life?
- How can I apply this concept?
- Does this concept fit?

Come up with multiple answers. See the human in every interpretation. We don't have to feel bad if we don't agree with every word we hear. We also don't have to judge the person we are disagreeing with as right or wrong. We simply can say things like:

- *That hasn't proven true in my life.*
- *I see things differently, but I'm not saying your way is wrong.*

- *This is what works best for me in my life...I'm happy you've found a way that works well in yours.*

PERSPECTIVE OF EMPOWERMENT...

To My Vision through Perspective,

The understanding of perspective is the power that sets me free. It's what helps me to see that my feelings and thoughts are the only things that create love or war within me. I can choose to believe in whatever I want to. If that perspective of thought hurts me, I'm responsible for choosing to continue the thinking that keeps me in darkness or to embrace thinking that brings me into the light. No one can get into my head—only I live there. Other people can only feed the love or fear that I'm letting them feed.

I'm choosing to see my life through the perspective of love. Believing in this perspective is a personal decision. It's not my business what other people think about the perspectives I choose to live by. It's not my business if people believe what I say or not. Only they can make the choice of what perspectives they want to live by. If they live in fear of mine, they will attack me, but really the person they are attacking is him/herself. I can't make them feel anything, just like they can't be responsible for anything I feel. I can choose to see my traumatic experiences as blessings. I can choose to forgive any and all people whose actions caused me pain. Those are my choices based on my perspectives of belief. That doesn't mean they are the choices another person has to make.

The blessings and consequences of their choices are on them. My power is what I choose for me.

I am responsible for my vision. When I see humanity through perspectives of truth instead of right and wrong, I remain open to learn and grow in love. If I insist on my own way, it means my attachment to a belief has become unhealthy, and I start feeding fear and the violence within me as I try to defend my beliefs and my actions. I believe I need to be the best version of myself. In that vision, I grow into being a better me. I become an authentic me who accepts and appreciates authentic encounters with others.

As I grow in my vision, I commit to asking more questions. I want to be able to see more of the love the world has to offer. My goal in my connection to others is to see the love within them, no matter what they choose to believe. This view keeps me focused on truly loving my neighbor as I love myself. My perspective to live from a loving place is clear. Through this vision I see the empowered woman I am. I commit to being part of transforming the world.

With Love and Gratitude,

The Empowered Woman

SEEING THROUGH EYES OF PERSPECTIVE

In the end, everything boils down to perspective. Seeing life through perspectives of truth keeps us open to better ourselves, communicate with others, and make positive changes in the world. Since the beginning of the book, you have been engaging in one perspective after another, whether you embraced the beliefs you were reading or were inflamed with anger by them. We get to choose what feels right and what doesn't. As they say in Al-Anon, "Take what you like and leave the rest." Being the empowered woman that you are, you get to choose how you will react, feel, think, and believe after reading this book. You get this choice in every situation you encounter. We embrace our own empowered woman when we stop giving our power away. Being clear about our own perspectives of thinking is an essential step in discovering our authentic selves and serving with authenticity. This is how we transform the world.

In my perspective, love is not righteous. I know I'm truly moved when I can't stop taking notes connecting to the love within me and to others. I feel tingles run throughout my body as I feel the truth behind the words and actions. When I open myself up to believe in possibilities, I hear the beautiful messages of people who may think differently than me and have their own way of experiencing authentic love. I know from my experience of family that we all have different ways of looking at life. No two people think exactly the same. I see the blessings in that. By looking at life through the vision of perspective, we're open to change and grow without resistance from generations of old beliefs that no longer serve us.

Feed the empowered woman that you are. Treat her with the love and respect that you are giving to others. Be true to the perspectives that bring you peace, love, compassion, and empathy for yourself and others. Set better-me goals.

How do you want to see your internal world as you grow into a better version of yourself?

Create an action plan. What are some daily actions you can take to achieve these goals? We can make the changes we want to see in the world by becoming the change. We are empowered! It's our choice to embrace our internal empowered woman or not. My prayers go out to all the women on this journey of discovery. Let the guiding force of love be with you.

GOING DEEPER

Practice perspective. Take any situation in your life and come up with different ways to look at it. Don't think of right or wrong answers, just look at different perspectives. Do this in short spurts, just whenever you think about it. When we do this, we become open to seeing our perspective as a choice. This exercise will help you grow and expand in your communication with others. It's *mind-blowing*!

ONE FINAL LETTER...

Dear Reader,

Thank you for taking this journey with me. These are seeds from my garden. I was given these throughout the years and chose to plant them. My life is a reflection of the seeds I chose to plant. It is your choice to do what you want with the seeds you take away from this book. Whatever you choose, I hope you love and maintain your foundation, so that you may create your inner garden from a loving place and be the positive change in your own internal world and for the world around you. If this book encourages you to want to take action, here's a challenge for you. Buy copies to give to your local women's organizations. Spread the love. Remember, if you choose this challenge, do it because you feel called to do it, not because you think you should. If you're not called to do it—don't do it. See how the thought of doing it makes you feel. Listen to the empowered woman inside you.

Take action today! What can you do right in this moment to do your part in transforming the world?

To go even deeper with more letters and exercises, visit FromALovingPlace.com and choose the category "How Becoming an Empowered Woman Transforms the World."

With Immense Love and Overwhelming Gratitude,

Rachael Wolff

FINAL THOUGHTS TO PONDER

I started Part II with a quote from Byron Katie: "The most attractive thing about the Buddha was that he saved one person: himself. That's all he needed to save; when he saved himself, he saved the whole world." As you read the quote now, take time to sit down and ponder:

- Does the quote above hold more power?
- Have I noticed any energy shifts since I started reading this book?
- Have I noticed shifts in my perception?
- Have I noticed people around me changing?
- Do these changes inspire me to invest time in myself?
- Am I ready to see the light my positive worth can create?
- Am I ready to change the world?

In order to create positive change in the world, we have to see ourselves with clarity. Don't stop doing the work. Keep your light shining! Continue to invest in staying aware, accepting what is, and taking action to make today better.

Acknowledgments

When I think about all the people it took for me to write this book, I become overwhelmed with joy. Just writing these words, I feel the tears starting to form in my eyes. I want to start from the beginning. My mom (Mary) and dad (Paul) showed the rewards and consequences of living in love versus fear. Through watching them, I learned how people can change and grow when they get out of their own way. My sister (Rebecca) is my example of how we can live under the same roof, grow up under the same conditions, and have different memories, thoughts, and experiences that guide our own perspectives of truth. She also qualifies as the best sister ever. My oldest friend (Chessa) has shown me a high level of courage, bravery, and strength, mixed with a lot of learning experiences. My high school guidance counselor (Norma) kept showing me light until I could see my own.

Each life experience has played a part in this book, so all the people who have touched my life are a part of my garden. I'm blessed to have an amazing extended family who taught me a great deal about loving people through our differences. I've had so many extraordinary friendships that there really are too many to mention. My stepdad (Carl) and my special mom (Joyce) both have played significant roles in my life, showing me what my parents looked like when they lived with their partners from a loving place and how that transformed all our relationships. At the young age of fourteen, I was introduced to Marianne Williamson's book, *A Return to Love*. This book was the beginning of a lifelong journey toward igniting the fire in my heart. The relationships that didn't work out taught me about my boundaries, my codependency, my weaknesses, and my strengths, along with how my perspective needed to shift in order for me to grow, change, and transform into the person I am today.

The two best things that came from any life lesson are my children (Aidan and Alyssa). I learn so much through my love for them about the person I am and the person I strive to be. They give me the greatest lessons about the importance of not taking things personally and how someone else's choices are not my responsibility (LOL). I also get endless lessons in love, accountability, and responsibility. My love for them is what drove me to dive into the journey of becoming the best me I possibly can.

My experience at Eckerd College as a newly single mom led the way to each and every one of these pages being written. Through my college experience, professors, classes, friends, and endless papers, I built the confidence I needed to invite the outside world into my perspectives of love and hope. My professor in the creative process (Marta Davidovich Ockuly, PhD) has remained my mentor and inspiration through the process of writing this book.

FromALovingPlace.com followers, readers, and supporters were unknowing participants in helping me find my voice for this book. It was through my blogging that the concept of *Letters From a Better Me* was developed. Sheila Burke sharing my first letter on her BeingBetterHumans.com page was the seed planted for me to write a book. Damien Thomas asking me to write a couple of pieces for his site, YourPositiveOasis.com, showed me that people connected to my voice and style of writing. The comments and likes from followers inspired me to keep going.

With a few amazing people, including my mom, stepdad, and my wonderful partner in love (Zeke), I was able to dedicate my time to writing this book without having it take away from my time being the parent I wanted be. Yes, the tears are rolling now. Thank you for being the example of the power of love and the many blessings that come with opening my heart to what is. Zeke stayed my cheerleader even when my light started to dim.

If there was one friendship that has taught me the most about the Universe, it's the one I have with my soul sister and agent (Tina Wainscott). We started out as neighbors over a decade ago and have been inseparable ever since. Writing this particular book came from her question, "Do you think you could write a book on women's empowerment?" Our trip to Sedona, Arizona, led me to say, "I think I figured out how I can." From that point on, it's been a whirlwind. She has been with me *every* step of the way. It was her vision of the book finding the right editor and publisher that kept pushing me through what felt like the endless sea of the most beautiful passes.

This brings me to the talented Brenda Knight from Mango Publishing, who saw a vision for this book and, despite my limited social media following, brought it to the Mango team and helped them to see her vision clearly. I'm so grateful for the chance to prove the Mango Publishing team right in their decision! I'm grateful to Lisa Goich for supporting the cause of empowering women and writing the beautiful foreword to this book. A special thanks goes out to all the *amazing* women who endorsed the book.

Lastly, I thank the tribe of women that I have not mentioned yet who bring smiles, laughs, tears, and joy to my life: Autumn, Stephanie, Erin, Gena, Janeanne, Jenn, Kris, Kaya, Lily, Terry Anne, Sandra, Kendra, Barbara, Marie, Lena, Jeni, Sonya, Carolyn, Chrissy, Melissa, Nicole, Dana, Lois, Danielle, Annie, Kristie, Kim, and Bonnie (for all your help with my kids), along with so many more. Surrounding myself with these women encourages me to keep shining.

About the Author

Rachael Wolff is the creator and facilitator of the "35-Day A Better Me Boot Camp" and the "90-Day A Better Me Series" offered on her blog, FromALovingPlace.com. Wolff graduated from Eckerd College with a bachelor's degree in Human Development and a minor in Anthropology, focusing on cultural anthropology. After receiving her degree with an award in "Excellence in Human Development," she used her own thirty years of personal and spiritual development, along with her education, to fulfill her life's purpose of becoming a transformational coach. Her goal is to inspire individuals to make great changes in the world by becoming their best selves.

Follow her on social media:

Facebook.com/Lettersfromabetterme

Facebook.com/FromALovingPlace

Instagram.com/LettersfromABetterMe

Twitter.com@Wolff_Rachael

Mango Publishing, established in 2014, publishes an eclectic list of books by diverse authors—both new and established voices—on topics ranging from business, personal growth, women's empowerment, LGBTQ studies, health, and spirituality to history, popular culture, time management, decluttering, lifestyle, mental wellness, aging, and sustainable living. We were recently named 2019's #1 fastest-growing independent publisher by *Publishers Weekly*. Our success is driven by our main goal, which is to publish high-quality books that will entertain readers as well as make a positive difference in their lives.

Our readers are our most important resource; we value your input, suggestions, and ideas. We'd love to hear from you—after all, we are publishing books for you!

Please stay in touch with us and follow us at:

Facebook: Mango Publishing

Twitter: @MangoPublishing

Instagram: @MangoPublishing

LinkedIn: Mango Publishing

Pinterest: Mango Publishing

Sign up for our newsletter at www.mangopublishinggroup. com and receive a free book!

Join us on Mango's journey to reinvent publishing, one book at a time.